Clarity
is the only
Spirituality

Susunaga Weeraperuma

BEL!EF

Reprint 2023

FiNGERPRINT! **BEL!EF**
An imprint of Prakash Books India Pvt. Ltd.

113/A, Darya Ganj, New Delhi-110 002,
Tel: (011) 2324 7062 – 65, Fax: (011) 2324 6975
Email: info@prakashbooks.com/sales@prakashbooks.com

facebook www.facebook.com/fingerprintpublishing
twitter www.twitter.com/FingerprintP
www.fingerprintpublishing.com

ISBN: 978 93 8777 903 7

Processed & printed in India

DEDICATED TO
THOSE WHO VALUE
CLEAR-SIGHTEDNESS
AND THE ENSUING
GOODNESS OF HEART

CONTENTS

1
CLARITY IS
THE ONLY
SPIRITUALITY

I wanted to write a short essay about what needs to be done in order to develop the ability to think clearly and perceive correctly without any distortion whatsoever.

With this intention in mind, I sit at my desk on a quiet summer morning. The light outside is bright. The conditions seem just right for me to carry out my intended investigation, but I find that the temperature is too high for my liking. It is difficult to concentrate. So, I switch on the fan and wait for it to cool my study. Even so, I realise that I have to struggle to focus my mind on the task at hand. Then, it dawns on me that it is nothing but my restless and wandering mind that prevents me from getting down to work. The problem, clearly, is purely psychological in origin.

While I am keen to write about the importance of clear thinking, every time I actually try to do that, my attention gets easily distracted. There is always something else that occupies the mind. Why I wonder, is my interest in this topic not as overpoweringly engaging as to outshine all other interests and distractions?

I try again to write when, lo and behold, I want to respond to Martin's letter first! Then, the very next moment, it occurs to me that his letter does not actually warrant a reply, it being a reply to one of my previous letters! Having disposed of that distraction, I try, yet again, to get on with my essay, only to immediately remember that the two recently planted apple trees have to be watered now, especially because their leaves look a little wrinkled and withered. But I postpone the garden work until sunset, heeding farmers' advice that early mornings and late evenings are the best times for watering plants. Having successfully handled two distractions, I am glad to be able, at last, to commence work. But, no sooner have I lifted my pen to write than the phone starts ringing. I decide not to answer the call. It rings for three full minutes before it stops.

Whenever you are *fully aware* of the existence of distractions, they no longer cause trouble; they cease having a stranglehold on you. Once you become *alert* to the distractions, they stop being distractions. Hence the supreme importance of *constant alertness and vigilance.*

With the help of a pencil sharpener, one can quickly and very easily sharpen a pencil. But is there just as quick and easy a method of sharpening the mind and making it capable of great clarity? One doubts if clarity can be obtained by doing anything wilfully. But clarity *is* realisable by means of *via negativa.*

The term *via negativa* needs explanation. What is the sensible thing to do when your pet dog's dirty footprints have discoloured your white carpet? Some would apply white paint to cover up the stains instead of simply washing them off with water. Given the conditioned state of the mind with its ingrained prejudices and greedy dispositions, we are incapable of transforming ourselves. We can no more change ourselves than we can lift up our bodies with our shoelaces. But once we become *aware* of our negative traits, doing so by means of meditation, what happens? The negative traits disappear and the positive ones spring into action of their own accord. When, for instance, the mean and stingy traits drop off from the mind, it is automatically replete with goodness and generosity. The negation of the bad results in the inevitable emergence of the good. This is the negative path to spirituality, also called *via negativa*. If you avoid doing anything that stands in the way of clarity, eschewing confusion and obscurity, you find it indirectly.

One day, I was reading a newspaper in a library when I was disturbed by some readers' loud conversation.

"Please be quiet," I requested them. "I can't give my attention to what I'm reading."

"Do you really have to pay attention to what you're reading when it's merely a newspaper?" one of them retorted.

"Whatever I do, I give it my *undivided attention*," I explained.

They ignored what I said and continued to talk. *O tempora! O mores!* — O the times! O the customs!

What happens when one gives one's undivided attention to all of one's activities? What are the consequences of being fully attentive, as opposed to being partially perceptive?

Those who give total attention, quite obviously, tend to make fewer mistakes than those who do not. They are, for instance, less likely to be run over and killed by a vehicle when crossing the road. They also learn more and gather more information than those who are inattentive. Because they are mentally alert, they become capable of detecting their shortcomings, prejudices, fears, and hidden frustrations far more quickly than those who are mentally lethargic. They have, therefore, a better chance of developing their capacity to think clearly. Besides, the fully attentive generate a certain intensity which is indispensable for spiritual advancement.

Unless one is fully attentive, is it possible to detect the cunning ways of the mind, the significance of dreams, the subtle tricks and secrets of the unconscious? Without being totally alert, will it ever be possible to uncover the hidden side of one's own self? And what is one without self-knowledge?

Even far back in time, the ancient Greeks valued self-knowledge. One of J. Krishnamurti's favourite sayings is that self-knowledge is the beginning of wisdom. Reading a great many books and acquiring a plethora of academic qualifications might help one get a good job and prosper in society, but it is absolutely necessary to distinguish between academic knowledge and self-knowledge.

Self-knowledge is nothing more than the psychological luggage that always accompanies one. Principally, self-knowledge consists of all the subtle workings of one's mind, which one discovers by fits and starts, but never fully. It is the information about oneself that one is ashamed to reveal to outsiders. Aching frustrations, disappointments in love, failures in getting the desired jobs, poor performance in certain examinations, jealousies of persons who have done better, conflicts with family members—all these factors influence one's thinking as well as one's reactions to things, persons, and ideas.

The gathering of self-knowledge is something that even an illiterate person can do. But one must not, for that reason, undervalue self-knowledge. For without it, would we not continue being proud and domineering? Would we not be spiritually handicapped?

To go past the gates of spirituality, one should be clear-headed. Muddle-headed folk get stuck in the mud of ignorance and stagnate in *samsara*, suffering indefinitely in a cycle of miserable births and deaths.

Many so-called religious persons are not clear about what constitutes spirituality. Here again, one must opt for *via negativa*, discarding one by one those practices that are stumbling blocks to genuine spirituality, having defined spirituality as clearness of mind or clarity of thought.

Often, those who are very old or critically ill, suddenly become religious. Similarly, those who are going through an emotional crisis also turn to religion sometimes. These people are mistakenly termed 'religious' or 'spiritual', whereas in reality, they are only desperately seeking sympathy, comfort, help, and consolation.

But genuine spirituality is the search for Truth, the eternal verities. It is *not* the search for happiness. The truth about oneself, warts and all, can be most disturbing. How many of us are really prepared to face facts and see ourselves exactly as we are, viewing all our negative tendencies in the mirror of awareness? This, no doubt, will be most unsettling as we have such an exalted opinion of ourselves. And looking into such a mirror would go against our grain to seek happiness at all times and to never do anything that might cause the slightest unhappiness. If only we had the honesty to look at ourselves without any distortion! Only a clear-sighted person can distinguish between those who regard religion as a form of escape from the burdens and problems of life, and those who see religion as a serious quest for Truth.

A mind that is full of prejudices is incapable of clear thinking. But, there are a multitude of racial and religious prejudices in almost every society today. Our prejudices are created by having particular images and preconceived ideas about individuals belonging to certain groups. They are created and reinforced through stereotypes. Why do we view others through the images of our own making? Why do we fail to see that these images poison our minds against our fellow humans? Is it ethically right to brand human beings as 'stingy Jews', 'Islamic terrorists', 'dirty Arabs', 'coloured people', 'white people' and so forth? If only we could realise how our prejudices are responsible for all the unnecessary divisions in the world!

Even learned scholars often fail to see how images distort perception. We have made ourselves incapable of seeing *anew* and *afresh* not only those who we know well, but also those who we do not know at all. Why do we carry with us mental photographs of people that do not correspond with what they actually look like now? Are we not, as a result of this horrible habit, naturally getting a skewed and inaccurate version of reality?

The word 'awareness' is frequently used to describe the detached, impartial, and non-judgemental observation of one's thought processes. It is done without condemnation or approval of the numerous feelings and thoughts that flash through the mind. It is self-observation at its best.

Instead of habitually turning our attention outwards, we can, for once, turn it inwards to discover that which is hidden within us. As we become conscious of the workings of both the conscious and the unconscious, we invariably begin to discover ourselves as we truly are. By giving the unconscious full rein, by opening the floodgates of the mind, we often come to know ourselves in a surprising way.

A do-gooder who is fully aware of his thoughts and feelings, for example, might unearth the truth that the underlying reason for his philanthropy is the eagerness to cover up his essential stinginess. This realisation will be such a shock to his system that he might spontaneously and effortlessly drop his stinginess. Thereafter, as a consequence of this insight, he might become a genuinely generous gentleman. Such changes of heart, rare as they are, occur as a result of self-awareness or self-observation. They are the reward for being suffused with clarity.

Clear thinking or clarity is a frequent concomitant of awareness. Here, let us consider the work done by judges. It is absolutely necessary that judges should be intensely aware of their thought processes. Those judges who succeed in detecting their aversions, will become so cautious in their thinking that they will not allow themselves to be influenced by their hitherto hidden dislikes. Once a judge knows, for instance, that he detests thieves, especially because his car had been stolen, he will avoid giving a harsh sentence to a starving, unemployed man who has committed a credit-card fraud.

Long ago, I worked in an office where the principal shortcoming of the boss was his promiscuous sexual behaviour. His bias towards female employees in the organisation resulted in his giving promotions only to attractive women. But, as a result of right meditation involving inner awareness, he suddenly dropped his shameful, discriminatory policy and began giving promotions only to deserving employees, regardless of their gender. It is awareness that enabled him to think clearly and turn over a new leaf.

From time immemorial, there have been religions with various moral codes. Extraordinary and exemplary religious teachers like the Buddha, Jesus, Mahavira, and Zarathustra, and a few of their disciples, delved deeply into themselves and discovered things that enriched civilisation. Yet, regrettably, through the ages, millions have remained largely unaffected by their moral, philosophical, and religious teachings.

Man is still, essentially a beast at heart. For example, the modern man's passion for violent sports like boxing is not fundamentally different from that of the ancient Romans' desire to see Christian martyrs being torn asunder by wild animals in the Colosseum. Has the primitive nature of man not changed at all? Why have we failed to change despite our rich religious legacy? Where have we gone wrong? Have any of our current religious practices helped to bring about a fundamental change in the animalistic nature of man?

People often ask if studying the sacred scriptures of different religions precipitates a fundamental change in the human psyche or not. While such religious studies might result in one becoming a scholar, they might not necessarily result in a spiritually illumined saint. Anyone who is well-versed in comparative religion can share that knowledge with his students in schools and universities. This will broaden the outlook of the younger generation and check their tendency to think that their parental religion is the only good religion, if not the best.

Also, sacred scriptures are often couched in elegant and elevated language. If nothing else, reading religious texts would at least appeal to one's sense of beauty!

A study of different sacred scriptures would also be a good training for the priesthood. When priests know about other faiths, they might just become less fanatical about their own religion.

But when all is said and done, while religious knowledge has its place, it can never be a substitute for self-knowledge, which alone is the path to spiritual liberation.

It is also often assumed that pilgrimages to sacred places could help hasten the process of a spiritual metamorphosis. Over the years, I have visited several important religious centres that are frequented by thousands of pilgrims, notably Lourdes in France, Fatima in Portugal, Bodh Gaya in India, and Medjugorje in Bosnia-Herzegovina. I went out of curiosity to observe the behaviour of pilgrims and to absorb the special atmosphere of these places. My journeys to these religious sites were neither expressions of faith nor longings to find miraculous cures for my minor ailments, although at Lourdes I did intercede with Our Lady on behalf of friends who were critically ill.

What I learned after these journeys was that while pilgrimages do reinforce the religious faith of some, unfortunately, their psychological traits continue to remain the same. Alas, no great religious transformation takes place. That is to say, even after a religious expedition which often involves considerable expense, physical fatigue, and other inconveniences, their grudges remain raw and open, like unhealed wounds.

After a short pilgrimage to Mecca, a person I knew

came back with a holier-than-thou attitude. When I started ignoring her haughty manner, she took revenge by no longer being friendly towards me. Of what use then are pilgrimages that strengthen egos instead of eliminating them altogether?

If not pilgrimages, then people take to fasting, prayer, and penance. But they hardly stop to think whether such practices are a help or hindrance to real enlightenment.

When you are ready, Truth will come to you. One cannot pursue Truth or obtain it as though it were a thing for sale in the marketplace. Do what you want, for the Supreme cannot be reached by any act of yours or by any exercise of will. Will is the arm of the 'I'; it springs from the ego. But if and when the mind is unconditioned and the nasty 'I' is therefore no more, there is a possibility of the Unconditioned blossoming. When the cup is empty, it might happen. Our minds, however, are anything but vacant and unoccupied.

But instead of doing this, that and the other, for once, simply sit back and watch yourself, albeit in a passively alert manner. Just observe your thought process. Let your mind pour out all its contents. Allow it to cleanse itself of its self-centredness.

Now observe how your 'I', which is only a thought that tries foolishly to interfere with all the other thoughts and boss them around, is no more than a mere thought. When the 'I' tries to control the thought process, the ego strengthens itself, and then one is full of self-importance. But the 'I' is itself part of the thought process, even though it pretends to be a superior entity that likes to remain aloof from the constantly moving chain of thoughts. Both the 'I' and all the other thoughts together constitute the thought process. It is vitally important to understand this truth because all the so-called meditational systems in existence are caught in a trap where the 'I' or the 'thinker', strives hard to control, subjugate, and direct the course of the entire thought process!

Once the 'I' tries in any way to interfere with the thought process, what happens? There will be short periods of thought-free calm, but after a time, the thought process re-emerges from its suppressed state with redoubled vigour instead of disappearing once and for all. However, the moment you *fully understand* how you have hitherto been fooling yourself, that flash of clarity will enable you to disentangle yourself from your futile exercise. Thus ends this duel between thought and the thought-created 'thinker', the 'I' or the ego.

Unexpectedly, the mind is free then. Being replete with clarity, it effortlessly sheds its shackles. This clarity is the only spirituality. And out of the fountain of this spirituality, the healing waters of compassion start to shoot high up into the skies before spraying down onto every living being far below, doing so for the benefit of everything that breathes.

2

URGENCY OF RELIGIOUS TOLERANCE

Religions, instead of merging differing groups into one loving and harmonious whole, have split up the world into warring factions. This unfortunate situation is certainly not a reflection on the founders of the various religions who were, by and large, men of goodwill and extraordinary spiritual stature. Rather, it is a reflection of the nature of the times we live in.

There is a saying that religions were founded by laymen and corrupted by priests. This profound statement is worth pondering over again and again. Let us envisage for a moment, an enlightened society where the citizens are absolutely self-reliant in religious matters, thereby eradicating any need for a priest. In such a highly evolved community then, the poor priests would become unemployed! They would then, be rendered unable to misinterpret and corrupt the sacred religious scriptures!

Once, a clergyman was giving a speech at an open-air meeting, when a hostile member of the audience started to heckle him.

"Religions have existed for thousands of years, but look at the state of the world today!" exclaimed the heckler.

"Water has existed for thousands of years, but look at the state of your face!" retorted the man of the cloth.

At a superficial level, this looks like a witty repartee. But, there is more to that remark than meets the eye. Although religions have existed, in some form or the other, since the dawn of civilisation, it is man who, having failed to understand the very basic tenets of religion, naturally either misapplied them or failed to apply them at all. Why pin the blame on the Buddha, Christ, Krishna, Moses or Mohammed, when it clearly lies with us? It is we who did not drink the pure water that they offered.

"But were the waters that the masters gave us always clean and pure?" a person with an inquiring mind might ask.

All my life, I have been a student of comparative religion and philosophy. Often, when going through the pages of some sacred scripture or the other, much to my surprise, I have chanced upon passages that justify animal sacrifices, violence, killing, and even war. Such statements I reject outright, regarding them as pure fabrications, as the interpolations of religious zealots or others with powerful vested interests. They have, over the ages, surreptitiously changed the contents of books. This decision of mine to ignore or discard lines that are in conflict with the genuine spirit of what the great teachers taught is a purely personal and subjective one. When, for instance, I read statements ascribed to the Buddha wherein the killing of animals for food was permitted, I immediately question their authenticity. A few great teachers like the Buddha and Vardhamana Mahavira extolled the importance of *Ahimsa* (non-violence) and compassion for all living beings. There is absolutely no place in their teaching either for cruelty to living creatures or killing them for whatever purpose.

If I might use a cliché that expresses exactly what I wish to stress, I dislike throwing away the baby with the bath water. This means that I am willing to read, study, and follow any religious teaching, provided it is acceptable, reasonable, and not in any way contrary to the ethical principles that I uphold. Expressed differently, I gladly *tolerate* each and every religious text, regardless of the religious teacher who expounded it, so long as it is in accordance with *Sanatana Dharma*—the eternal ethical law.

In most societies, it has long been the practice for people to accept, without careful and thorough consideration, the religion of their parents. From our fathers and mothers, we tend to take automatically their prearranged sets of religious beliefs, dogmas, doctrines, ideas, and attitudes, including their aversions and prejudices. It is like inheriting property that once belonged to them. If you dare to disagree with those who brought you up, you risk the possibility of being treated with scorn.

Parents and schools can promote the cause of religious tolerance by urging the younger generation to read and study the religious writings of *all* religions, thereby enabling those under their charge to discover all that is good, wise, and wonderful in every religious tradition. For one thing, the youth will become not only well-read, but also broad-minded, and consequently, religious intolerance will soon become a thing of the past.

The educational systems in some parts of the world are heavily biased towards the study of science. This is the situation in France, with the result that a good many people love to scoff at religion and frequently equate it with superstition and the irrational. The French Revolution left a legacy of hatred and fear of religion. Secularism, as a result, has become the order of the day. But is it really possible to delve deeply into French civilisation by ignoring the nation's philosophy, art, architecture, and literature, which are all rooted in religion? Religion is the foundation of French civilisation and culture, whether or not the French wish to recognise that unpalatable fact.

Whenever an anti-religious person gives up his animosity towards people who are ardently religious, he not only becomes tolerant towards his former adversaries' views, but he also becomes warm-hearted, thereby discovering new friends. Jews and Muslims, for instance, will suddenly be on speaking terms. And once these hitherto hostile groups are on friendly terms, even nuclear disarmament becomes possible in the Middle East and elsewhere. The valuable resources of the world, scarce as they are, would no longer be wasted on senseless and useless wars. There will be more money available that can be used for the economic, educational, cultural, and social development of mankind.

As a consequence of religious tolerance, more and more people will want to study the religious writings of other cultures. Inevitably, everyone will soon realise that no particular religious group has a monopoly on truth. They will also see the utter folly of becoming fanatical about any religion. Then, our war-torn world will turn into a peaceful paradise.

But, urgent is the need for such a change in outlook, for we are now on the verge of mutual destruction. How can we bring about such a great change in our attitude to religion that we can transcend our current lethargy and sense of hopelessness? Is it possible through governmental action and legislation to make men and women see the importance of being tolerant in all matters relating to religion? No. It is becoming increasingly clear that no external agency, force, pressure or deity can help us to make a breakthrough. We have to act individually, and we have to do it alone. And is not the practice of religion a purely private matter? Since what one does in the name of religion is a personal affair, no government has the right to interfere in it. The state cannot anyway regulate what a person does in the privacy of his home. No state official can know or supervise what a person does behind closed doors. A government inspector can neither oversee the devotional chants and religious rituals of people nor probe into their minds to discover their loyalties, beliefs, and ideas.

People often make a show of their religious faith by

dressing in a certain way or behaving in such a manner as to draw attention to themselves and their faith. The ostensible reason for such behaviour is usually that they are only promoting their religion. But if they cared to examine themselves, they would probably find that it is their ego that is subtly clamouring to get some attention! And it doesn't stop here. They also make attempts to provoke people by making such statements or by conducting themselves in such a manner as to hurt the religious and moral sensibilities of those whose outlook on life might be different from their own!

Without collective action, it would not be possible to run a large factory or do all the work involved in keeping a farm running, from looking after the animals and the crops to tilling the land. But meditation, which is the impartial awareness of the ways of the mind, necessarily entails individual self-observation. It can only be done alone; it is not an activity that lends itself to being shared with another person.

If an intolerant state were to pass laws that prohibit people from meditating, such legislations could not be enforced. Similarly, should any state declare that it is illegal to pray, it will be beyond the bounds of possibility to make people obey it. Praying, which is a form of communion with the Divine, involves and concerns only two parties: the individual who prays and the Absolute.

"When you pray," instructed Jesus, "do not be like the hypocrites who love to stand and pray in the synagogues and street corners to be seen by others. But when you pray, enter your room and close its door."

Evidently, Jesus did not believe in congregational praying. One can surmise then that he would have frowned upon praying in a church unless the place was empty of people! He would have wanted us to pray in the privacy of our rooms, undisturbed by anyone or any noise, with no distractions, no prying eyes.

Once, I asked a Roman Catholic priest, who belonged to the religious order called Oblates of Mary Immaculate, the following question: "Father, do you think it's possible for a person to lead the Christian life without ever bothering to go to church?"

"Of course, it's possible," he answered with a smile.

Whenever a religion is practised in private, verbal or violent clashes between mutually distrustful religious groups can be avoided. However, there is one difficulty here. Only an insignificant minority of persons are keen on practising their religion in seclusion, in their homes and well away from the public eye. Devotees flock to temples, churches, mosques or synagogues in the expectation of satisfying their spiritual needs.

Even in secular nations like France, there is tolerance towards religious groups. Freedom of worship is part of the democratic way of life. The right to propagate one's religious beliefs, including the right to convert and proselytise, is also a part of the freedom of expression. But, there is a fine line between religious propagation and foisting one's beliefs on others and making a nuisance of oneself. The right to express oneself in public, either vocally or in the written form, should never be abused.

Some evangelical missionaries go from door to door, trying to talk you into accepting their sets of beliefs and thrusting their magazines and pamphlets into your hands. And they love to have arguments with you. They sincerely maintain that it is part of their religious discipline to take part in such activities. They say that they like to share with you their spiritual aspirations.

When they ring the bell to my home, often I do not know the best course of action to take. Sometimes I offer them cups of tea, but then they misuse the opportunity and prolong their visits. Sometimes I try to shatter their dogmas and make them see the light but all to no avail.

"Unless you accept Christ as the only saviour, you'll end up in hell!" they warn.

"Holy wars are justified by God," another one of them declared.

"Don't talk rubbish," I retorted with a touch of impatience. "He who does not love knows not God, for God is love."

"You're the one who's talking rubbish!" the man shouted back.

In this particular heated exchange, I am not sure which one of us, if any, was guilty of being intolerant. If I tell the evangelists that they are being intolerant, they turn the tables and accuse me of being intolerant of them!

When the bitter dispute eventually ends, I am thankful that they did not mercilessly put me to the sword, even though I am painfully conscious that I have been wasting my precious time. Nevertheless, exchanging ideas, I suppose, is better than exchanging blows!

In this connection, I recall an interesting conversation I once had years ago with a fellow reader in the British Museum Library. She was an American nun from the Bible Belt.

"Sir, you regard tolerance as a virtue, don't you?" she argued, brandishing her rosary. "Would you tolerate poison in your tea? I wouldn't."

"What's poison and what's nutrition will always be matters of personal opinion," I remarked.

"For me, atheism and agnosticism are two different kinds of poison," she continued. "I jolly well won't tolerate either."

What the nun said was food for thought. I, too, was inclined to agree with her, but only for a while. What seems like being dangerously venomous for some could turn out to be spiritual nectar for others, and vice versa. That, surely, is all the more reason why it is not only important but also incumbent upon each and every human being to be tolerant of divergent points of view.

Tolerance is the key to living peacefully in a world that is multi-religious, multiracial, and multicultural. Otherwise, we are doomed to disaster, conflict, and chaos.

3
IMPORTANCE
OF GOOD
COMMUNICATION

I live in the south of France where I meet all sorts of people. I regard this country as a microcosm of the whole world. Therefore, though my comments on human behaviour are naturally drawn on my French experiences, they are actually applicable everywhere, in any country, and it is the particular problems that I encounter in the course of everyday life here which have provided the main raw material for this essay.

"Can your observations on how people in one nation behave be generalised to those of the whole wide world?" a thoughtful person might ask. I take the point. But, despite the deep divergences that do exist between humans, I cannot overlook the fact that our psychological make-up is, more or less, the same *everywhere*, regardless of nationality, race, religion, age or gender. This finding is based on impressions that I have gathered during my travels around the world.

The opinions of people are noteworthy and what they have to say can be quite revealing. For example, a person's views on immigration might lead us to discover his or her xenophobia. I have, therefore, used false names to conceal the identity of people who feature in this discussion.

It goes without saying that good communication between people of different ethnic groups and of dissimilar religious sects is indispensable for maintaining peace and harmony in society. The delicate social fabric of any society begins to weaken and fray the moment the various communities that constitute this social unit stop having dealings with each other. If I am not on speaking terms with my neighbour, if I have bolted shut the door between us, isn't the situation similar to two countries breaking off diplomatic relations? No communication is possible anymore. I am incommunicado, which means that my neighbour cannot speak to me, even if he wishes to do so out of affection and good neighbourliness.

Imagine a scenario where a neighbour, who has recently become a religious fanatic, is determined to convert me to his religion.

"Unless you fully approve of my new faith and prayer practices, I'll have to treat you as a hostile unbeliever," he threatens. "This means there won't be any more friendly chats by the fence. Do I make myself clear?"

"But I'd like to examine your beliefs first and then decide whether to accept them or not," I plead with him.

"Examine my beliefs?! You don't have the intelligence to analyse these beliefs that are so well explained in our holy book," he argues while shaking his clenched fist in my face.

"Really?"

"If we can't agree," he continues, "then let's go our separate ways! Good riddance to bad rubbish, I say!" he mutters as he turns and walks away angrily.

My neighbour's cold-blooded severance of the cordial ties between us is painful. But worst of all, his single-mindedness prevents me from telling him my own point of view. If only he had given me the chance to tell him that instead of making a lifelong commitment to follow the dictates of just one book, no matter what it said, he could study the scriptures of other religions and develop a sense of spirituality of his own!

It is unfortunate that the French do not intermingle more freely with the Arabic-speaking Muslims who live and work in France. These Arabs, who are of North African origin, an estimated five million in number, never stop complaining that they are the victims of widespread racial and religious discrimination. In a similar vein, the French also protest that these Arab residents have failed to get integrated into French society. Whenever I hear complaints of such nature, I begin to think about the word '*intégration*', and how it is so often used against this large Muslim community in almost every Western European country. I have noticed that the people of this community are, on the whole, hard-working but not vociferous enough in their demands. They seem to accept their fate passively; it is difficult to motivate them to fight for their rights. More than content with their lot, most of them belong to the working class.

When it comes to religious matters or their settled way of living, however, the Arabs tend to be uncompromising. Religion is of central importance in their lives, especially if they are practising Muslims. The French, in contradiction, are largely indifferent to religion, which is not surprising given the fact that France is officially a secular country, and that except for a minority of practising Christians, the population, in general, seems to relish having anti-clerical and anti-religious attitudes. These particular attitudes are also fuelled by the smarting humiliation the French suffered as a consequence of the bitter Algerian fight for independence. In this strained setting, it is small wonder that both the French and the Muslim inhabitants of the country feel uneasy, anxious, and insecure and that their communication barely goes beyond a formal, feelingless "*Bonjour*".

One is puzzled then, by the concept of integration. Does it mean that the Arabs should become like the French or vice versa? But that will never happen! Ordinary mortals are too deeply rooted in their beliefs and ways of living to unlearn them. Then why don't we accept that there are great differences between all the various groups that inhabit the earth? What a dull world it would be if we were all alike! There is an urgent need to sustain a pluralist society where people of diverse religions, races, and ideologies can live together harmoniously. Following the establishment of such a community, will it not become easier for its citizens to communicate ideas, beliefs, and useful information with each other? Won't the exposure of people to these pluralist influences open their tightly closed minds?

Often, what is perceived as resentment towards our own selves on the part of a particular group of persons springs simply from our fear of them, which, in turn, is caused by our ignorance and lack of understanding of their culture. For instance, people in the West might harbour the fear that their culture, with its Christian roots, might someday be swept away and replaced by Islamic culture. The Muslims might be harbouring a similar fear of cultural, social, and religious displacement as well. But can anyone stop such a historical process from happening, if at all it ever will? What might probably occur is the synthesis or the blending of cultures, resulting in the emergence of a better, superior civilisation. Good communication, in such a scenario, can be the means to human evolution.

Bigotry and religious intolerance arise from our lack of knowledge of other religions. Therefore, the study of *all* the major religions of the world, and even the minor ones, should be an essential part of the curricula of all schools. And while progressive schools already have such programmes of study, most schools don't.

In fact, I wonder why people impose any specific religion on their children at all! Why not let them lead their lives in the light of what is *best* in *all* religions. When they come of age, can they not decide for themselves what religion, if any, they wish to follow? As a result of investigating comparative religion, they might want to accept only those faiths with such ethical values as appeal to their conscience and intelligence. They might, being utterly fed up with the senseless bloody wars of their forefathers, opt for religions that place a premium on non-violence and compassion even for those who swear by the sword.

None can accuse me of being hypocritical in this regard, for I have made a sincere effort to comprehend the culture and civilisation of the Arabs. I can honestly say that I do practise what I preach. From time to time Mekki, an Arab gardener, pays us a visit at our home and works his way through our garden. We, too, like to drop into his home to see how Mekki and his wife are getting on and ensure that they are in good health. They insist on serving us refreshments when we visit them. There is always an atmosphere of cordiality and informality in our relationship, which is quite a shock to many in our tiny town who like to keep this affable family at a distance!

Mekki is an exception in a world driven by insatiable avarice. Whenever he does strenuous work in our garden, I like to make a monetary payment, but the money I offer is invariably turned down.

"No, no," he cries out as I thrust the notes into his pocket. "You are me and I am you," he says. "We are one person with two separate bodies."

That remark could well have emanated from a Sufi or Hindu mystic. But my friend Mekki, a poor octogenarian, is a selfless man who likes to help *anyone* free of charge. It is all very well for him to decline the money, but has Mekki enough to pay for his day-to-day expenses? He is alone in a money-grabbing world.

The best way to discover the essential principles and elements of a people is to visit and live with them in the countries they inhabit. With this intention of stumbling upon the very soul of the Arabs, my wife, Claudia, who is of Swiss origin, and I have spent quite some time holidaying in two Arabic-speaking states—Tunisia and Morocco. In Marrakesh, we made friends with Abdel Kader Arabi and his wife, Khadija. Their hospitality touched our hearts. Subsequently, some of Claudia's poetry books and two of my novels were published by the Afaq Institute for Studies, Publication and Communication, which is owned by them. They awakened in us an interest in Arabic literature and Moroccan herbal medicine, which is the prevention and treatment of illnesses with local plants.

The second best method for interracial and interreligious communication is to read, study, and take delight in the literature of other communities. Fortunately for me, fine translations of many major Arab works are available. I have enjoyed reading the short stories and novels of Hanan Al-Shaykh who grew up in Beirut. I have also relished the writings of the Egyptian author Naguib Mahfouz, who was awarded the Nobel Prize for Literature in 1988, especially his fascinating novels that are set in Arab societies.

No survey of Arab literature is complete without an

appraisal of its most famous book, the *Koran*. The bibliophile in me has never failed to be impressed by the beautifully bound and frequently gilded versions of this sacred book. Several times, I have read the script of the *Koran* from cover to cover, struggling to find the meaning. However, I found it somewhat heavy going, mostly because of its lyrical and rhetorical style. Though interesting in itself, the *Koran* lends itself to being interpreted and understood in far more ways than one. Which way of viewing the lines is correct then? That, I am afraid, will always remain a purely personal and subjective matter. Consequently, over the centuries, many schools of thought on the subject have, quite inevitably, come into existence. Even for an Arabic scholar, the various meanings of the words in this text are fraught with interpretational problems. Given the hypersensitivity of this issue, the best course of action, as far as interpreting and dissecting the *Koran* are concerned, I feel, is to keep one's opinions to oneself and never openly or publicly express them. It is one of those rare situations in life when free and open communication can be dangerous. Remaining silent is the best policy. The right to communicate, in other words, is never absolute, and never a given.

Jean-Jacques Rousseau mourned the fact that although man is born free, he is everywhere in chains. We cannot act in any way we like, nor can we express ourselves freely, for what is said must not be offensive to other members of society. We are obliged to be careful to not offend others' susceptibilities, for it is possible that what one says inadvertently in private might be reported in the press, and then become world news, especially if one happens to be a political figure or a celebrity!

I realise now how odd it must read that I am cautioning the reader about the dangers of certain kinds of communication in an essay intended to promote more and more communication! But sometimes, careful and deliberate non-communication is what is needed. Sometimes, that is what can help a person out of harm's way.

It happened many years ago, while I was still living in Colombo. My father and I were sitting in the veranda of our home and having a chat one night when a pretty teenaged servant girl from a neighbouring house suddenly dashed into our portico. Dishevelled and looking panic-stricken, she was gasping for breath.

"Please allow me to hide under a bed, I beg you!" she cried.

"But why?" asked my father.

"My master wants to stab me with a knife," she said. "He wants to have sex with me, but I said no."

Without a word, we showed her the storeroom. She went inside and locked the door behind her.

My father and I returned to the veranda, wondering whether we had done the right thing or not by hiding that girl in our house. About thirty minutes later, our neighbour, a big, strong, middle-aged man, bare-bodied except for his green sarong and a white cap on his head, entered the veranda. He was holding a carving knife in his hand.

"Take a seat," said my father, not waiting for the man to explain his presence first. "Would you like some tea or coffee?"

"Maybe," the neighbour answered.

We noticed the wild expression on his face. This had to be the man the girl had told us about.

"Now make yourself at home," I said, slowly sliding out the weapon from his trembling hand and trying to disarm him. Actually, he sort of unconsciously released his grip on the knife and did not seem to mind what I was doing. Besides, we were already well acquainted with each other.

"Now, sir, tell us, what can we do for you?" asked my father.

"Have you seen my servant girl?" he inquired. "She has run away from my home because I scolded her for not working."

"In that case," said my father, "go immediately to the police station and tell them about her bad behaviour."

Thereupon, the man rose from his seat and left our home, forgetting to take away his knife. The following day, the girl expressed a keen desire to return to her parental home in a village. So my father gave her a few rupees for her bus fare and she left.

That night, by withholding the information the angry man sought, we probably averted a serious crime.

4

WRITE A
LETTER AND
FEEL BETTER

Several decades ago, when I was a young man, I used to receive at least a dozen handwritten letters each week. Today, however, receiving even one such letter during the course of a month is a cause of much marvel. The only letters I get now are official communications from government departments, bank statements, rejection letters from publishers, requests for monetary donations from charities, and flyers advertising this, that and the other. Why this dearth of personal letters, I wonder? Is it because I am seen now as an uninteresting oldie, no longer part of the productive workforce, no longer useful, no longer relevant? But that cannot be the reason because a lot of people who *are* part of the present-day workforce have told me that they do not receive personal letters either. What then, is the reason for the death of letters?

In fact, most people today don't even send letters of acknowledgement after receiving a present! It is rare indeed, that I get a letter of thanks in return for having sent a birthday or wedding gift to someone. The recipients of such gifts seldom seem to realise that the selection of a valuable and suitable gift often entails spending a lot of time and money. The least they can do is send a thank you note, one would think. It is not a question of wanting words of praise for the gift, not at all, but simply wishing to know whether it actually reached its destination or not, especially when so many packets go astray in the post every year. What a great pity that this long-cherished art of letter writing has come to such a sorry state! I hope it has not ended.

Recently, I was overjoyed to read in a newspaper that the widely acclaimed novelist Jhumpa Lahiri likes to read the published letters of writers who lived in bygone centuries, enthusiastically doing so for inspiration and pleasure. I have been entertained by the letters of D. H. Lawrence; some of them are absorbing travelogues. By going through such works, readers can not only learn about the lives of these writers, but also sit back and relax while becoming armchair travellers. It is often the case that more and more persons from the ageing population of the world lack the initiative and the stamina to have the real experience of travelling and seeing with their own eyes the far corners of the globe, like the polar regions for instance. Their failing health deters them from going to see exotic places in distant continents. But can they not entertain themselves by reading the vivid descriptions of idyllic settings trodden by the feet of literary men and women?

We are living in a world in which a large number

of people have inadequate communication skills even though, on the whole, they have had a reasonably good education. They've been to decent schools and colleges, and have acquired various diplomas. Yet, it appears, they cannot express themselves fluently, so much so that many universities have found it necessary to have intensive language courses for new entrants!

The educational systems of most nations are extremely lopsided. And this too, has played a role in the gradual death of the ancient and noble art of letter writing. The humanities, with their focus on the study of the classics, literature, philosophy, art, history, and the like, are regarded as being of secondary importance, whereas the sciences are deemed to be of primary importance. How then, will young people develop an understanding and appreciation of the finer nuances of life?

There was a time when essay writing occupied a place of honour in educational institutions throughout the world. Students were taught about the art of essay writing very early in life. Nowadays, however, the young gravitate towards the sciences, especially computer science, because the most remunerative jobs in our increasingly capitalistic societies are in this field. So, given the dearth of linguistic abilities and the dominance of economically-driven decisions, why wonder about the widespread reluctance to write letters or even reply to them?

Once, letters were a sign of being remembered, of being cared about. But the love and the concern people of previous generations had for one and all has unfortunately been replaced today by unbridled profit-driven selfishness. Most people, in other words, will now send or reply to a letter only if that would enable them to gain something. What they fail to realise is that by replying to a letter or sending one, they can at least retain the goodwill and friendship of the person receiving the letter. When you smile with satisfaction on hearing from the person to whom you had written, is that not a good enough reason to justify continuing to be in correspondence?

People fail to understand that the sum total of our seemingly insignificant acts of thoughtfulness can contribute not only to our private happiness, but to that of the entire community as well. But such is the enormity of our selfishness that we have hardly any time for reading about the trials and tribulations of another's life in their letters. Indifference is the order of the day.

"I am extremely busy now," is the usual excuse we give to shun our moral responsibility to concern ourselves with the lives of those around us. But why do we regard it as a great sacrifice on our part when it comes to devoting some time to learning about someone else's sufferings? Why do we not have a genuine interest in another's happiness and welfare? When and how did we ever become so focused on our own selves and blind to others?

I wish I could make others understand the power that a handwritten letter holds. I like to look carefully at the handwriting of a person I am corresponding with, but whom I have never seen or met, for even the sight of a few handwritten words is sufficient to get an insight into the character of the writer. The few people that I've come to know through the Internet remain faceless correspondents, like invisible spirits with the ability to send sudden and swift messages. No doubt, there are advantages to being able to correspond instantaneously with people sitting in another corner of the planet, but when it comes to delving deeply into a complex matter, I prefer old-fashioned letter writing. Pleasant is the touch and feel of written sheets of paper, after all, be they letters or printed books. Our behaviour can take an alarming and peculiar turn when our tactile sensations are deprived and cannot find expression.

The process of writing by hand, of putting down one's thoughts and feelings on paper, one word after the other, it takes time. It cannot and should not be rushed. It also needs a lot of patience. One should think twice about the words one chooses, lest one might regret them later. Letter writing forces one's quicksilver thought process to slow down, giving one the time and opportunity to consider all the implications, and especially, the wider aspects of any problem under discussion.

Mr. Rajan, a science teacher from Coimbatore in South India, was one of my several instructors when I studied at Mahinda College in Galle, which is an ancient and famous seaside resort town in Sri Lanka. Once, a fellow student sought the advice of Mr. Rajan during a weekly class devoted to a subject called General Knowledge. He complained that he was suffering from 'parentitis'. Never having heard of this condition before, Mr. Rajan asked him to describe the illness.

"Sir, parentitis is what one suffers from when one has a conflict with and harbours angry thoughts about one's parents," explained the worried youngster. "You see, father drinks a lot of arrack and then he beats me even if I haven't done anything wrong. I'm full of hatred towards my father, even though I know that as a Buddhist, what I'm doing is wrong. Yet, every day, I detest him more. How am I to cure myself of parentitis, sir?"

"Sit in a quiet place and write a long letter to your father," urged Mr. Rajan. "Write openly and tell him how difficult it has become for you to love him. Describe how you feel. Tell him, without any fear, that you hate him when he hits you for no apparent reason. Say that you're filled with anger as he doesn't treat you in a loving way. After you've written the letter, just wait for a few hours. You'll find that you've calmed down. And once you're at peace with yourself, you can tear up the letter," advised Mr. Rajan.

"But shouldn't I post it?" asked the boy, perplexed.

"No," replied Mr. Rajan. "No need to send the letter because by writing it, you've given vent to your spleen."

In certain circumstances, as Mr. Rajan made it clear to us that day, writing a letter of this kind can be of great therapeutic value. If the boy was ever thrashed again, the poor fellow would have had to grin and bear it, but at least he would have borne no malice towards his father. And perhaps he would have eventually reached a point where he no longer disliked his father ... wouldn't that be something?

Over the course of time, a former English teacher from my school became my lifelong friend and soul mate. We lived on different continents, but the great distance between us never stood in the way of our having an animated correspondence that lasted for three decades.

Looking back now, I realise that when writing a letter, it is best to only touch on subjects of mutual interest, otherwise one takes the risk of boring the recipient, and even putting the friendship in jeopardy! But more importantly, both the sides involved in the correspondence should feel free to write anything, provided it is true and sincerely felt and the nature of the relationship permits such honesty. This can be done effectively only when you have succeeded in losing your inhibitions. My friend, for instance, would write quite frankly about his love affairs, not leaving out details of his conflicts and misunderstandings with his lovers. He always told me how immensely relieved he felt after every letter that he wrote to me. Each letter was sort of a cathartic experience for him, a confessional perhaps. Mahatma Gandhi too, believed in the importance of making clean confessions. When he was a boy, he stole a few times. But, after realising what he had done was wrong, Gandhi resolved never to steal again. Then, he decided to confess his thieving to his father. So he wrote about it on a slip of paper and gave it to his father, asking for his forgiveness and also for adequate punishment for his misbehaviour. Trembling and scared, he handed the confession to his father who was ill and confined to bed. But after reading through it, tears trickled down his father's cheeks, wetting the paper. It was those pearl-drops of love that cleansed his heart and washed away his sin, not angry words of recrimination. This incident is reported in Gandhi's *An Autobiography or the Story of My Experiments with Truth.*

Those with a guilt-ridden conscience often seek mental relief by means of confessing their wrong-doings to a trusted friend or priest. As happened with Gandhi, the effectiveness of unburdening the mind depends not so much on the spiritual standing of the person who hears the confession, as it does on the open-mindedness and truthfulness of the troubled individual who *makes* the confession. This was the case with St Augustine's *Confessions.* In fact, it may sound silly, but it occurs to me that if a man makes an *honest* and *heartfelt* confession to a lamp-post or a tree for that matter, he can still find the same solace and comfort as he would by disclosing his moral misbehaviour to a man or woman of the cloth!

And, by the same token, if he finds no one willing to listen to his confessions, can he not turn inwards and *fully* admit to himself his moral lapses? Would such a course of action not be in accord with the path of self-knowledge and self-reliance? An individual who is inwardly watchful will never feel the need to seek out another person for the sake of making confessions.

But, I am digressing. Therefore, getting back to the

lost art of letter writing, great works of literature have been written in the form of letters addressed to specific individuals. The names of a few such books come into my mind. These publications have not only been famous and highly treasured, but are also extremely influential in the sense that they did change the way people thought. These consciousness-raising books left their mark on our culture.

Franz Kafka's *Letter to His Father*, for example, begins with a simple line. His father has recently asked him a question: Why does Franz maintain that he is afraid of him? Answering that simple inquiry entailed the writing of an entire book of considerable literary value. It involved going into the interesting complications of Kafka's inner life. Often, Kafka complains of his father's domineering personality and his thoughts and words inflicting suffering and shame on him. He also protests against his father's methods of upbringing. Once done writing the letter, Kafka gave it to his mother to hand it over to his father, hoping that it might result in a renewed and cordial relationship between them. But Kafka's mother, wanting to protect her husband, did not deliver the letter to her husband, instead, she returned it to him. Despite the fact that Kafka's attitude to his father remained unchanged, even after writing it, the letter, which, among other subjects, discusses Judaism at length, is remembered as a great contribution to German literature.

Another influential epistolary book is Jawaharlal Nehru's *Glimpses of World History*, which he wrote while he was serving his sentence in jail during India's freedom struggle. The letters in the book, while talking about major historical events, are addressed to his daughter. Written in a simple style for his only offspring, the book is of great interest and value even to adults and the general reader. Descriptions of places of historical importance that he visited are intermingled with his yearning for Indian independence.

One of the most elegantly written books I have read is *Letters to His Son* by Philip Stanhope. The 18th century writer of this classic, also known as the Fourth Earl of Chesterfield, instructs his son in this book, on how to behave and what to say in polite society. Out of affection for his son, he conveys to him the things he had learned about social life, good manners, and hygiene. The book is useful for anyone who wants to know and understand the inner workings of upper-class English society. Stanhope's *Letters to His Son* also shows us that collections of letters on specific subjects can be used for the production of excellent books of lasting interest.

A good example of a spiritual letter pertaining to the sublime is *Nagarjuna's Letter to King Gautamiputra*. The eminent Buddhist philosopher, Nagarjuna, sent this letter to his friend and patron, Gautamiputra, who was the king of Andhra in South India at that time. The letter consists of 123 verses that explain the fundamentals of Buddha's teachings.

Ours is an unhappy world, and nice letters can only lift our spirits. Therefore, there is an urgent need to revive this dying custom of letter writing. Any increase in the personal and intimate exchange of ideas and information will be a definite plus. The more letters we receive from our correspondents, the deeper becomes our insight into their hearts and minds, which, in turn, will result in better understanding and mutual affection.

5
VIRTUE OF
FORGIVENESS

One can quote numerous lines from sacred literature that extol the virtue of forgiveness. We cannot question the fact that there cannot be lasting peace and harmony in any society if its inhabitants are not ready and willing to forgive even those who are hell-bent on harming them. But how many, in all honesty, have the goodness to let go of resentment and anger against their adversaries? It is very easy to preach the virtue of forgiveness, but so difficult to express it in practical terms.

I once knew a girl called Sarah, a cute little child of mixed European and Asian descent. Her parents, very well-to-do people, were good friends of mine. Whenever I visited them, I would notice how they doted on Sarah, their only child and heiress. They would never tire of regaling me with stories of their daughter's beauty and intelligence. They expected her to become an influential socialite once she grew up. But, as fate would have it, everything came crashing down when Sarah's father died a tragic death in a car crash. Unprepared for such a turn of events, Sarah's mother took on the responsibility of single-handedly bringing Sarah up, albeit, with great reluctance. A little while after this upheaval, Sarah's mother fell for a prosperous businessman, and she soon deserted her own daughter and decided to live overseas with her newly found lover. Thereafter, poor Sarah was raised in a state-owned home for abandoned children.

About ten years later, I was doing my weekly shopping in a London supermarket when a young woman, fair-complexioned and dark-haired, approached me. "Do you remember me?" she asked. "I'm Sarah."

"Sarah!" I stared at the girl in front of me, totally surprised. "Ah! I would've never recognised you if you hadn't introduced yourself! How are you?"

"I clean other people's houses and shops," she replied with a bitter expression on her face. "I earn enough . . . so I'm not unhappy."

But she looked miserable. The years had clearly taken a toll on the girl.

"Any news of your mum?" I inquired.

"I stay away from that bitch," she snarled, grinding her teeth. "I can never forgive her for doing what she did, for abandoning me and ruining my life!"

Sarah's anger is not unjustified. But is there any person in this world who has not suffered the injustices of life? We all have our own lists of injustices and grievances. We are hurt when we are unfairly passed over for promotion; when our partner or spouse is unfaithful to us; when we are wrongly accused of committing a crime; parents are full of angst when their ungrateful children fail to take care of them when they are sick or aged; refugees from foreign lands feel insecure and traumatised when they are discriminated against because of their race, religion, colour, beliefs or political views. Our grievances are like psychological wounds. If we fail to heal these inner injuries with the balm of intelligence and understanding, then these mental mutilations will deepen and gnaw away at our peace of mind. But what exactly is one to do? Who has the time, energy or motivation to take up arms and fight a seemingly endless battle against every single act of injustice, no matter how small or big? So might it not be more sensible and prudent to forgive and forget instead?

Forgiveness is double-sided. On one hand, those who have been victimised, for whatever reason, must strive to try and forgive those who treated them badly in lieu of bearing grudges against them. On the other hand, if you are the wrongdoer, then can you not ask for forgiveness?

An act of forgiveness will be true and genuine only when it is asked for in a spirit of truly felt sadness at the misdeed. Simply saying "I am sorry" is not enough unless it is backed by feelings of honest regret. Feeling sincerely sorry for a wrongful deed is the element that purifies the mind. It allows one to be finally free of the guilt.

Some people think that merely asking for forgiveness is not enough. "Please forgive me" is only a psychologically soothing set of words. They maintain that compensation should, therefore, be expressed in a tangible form. Believing in this intangible quality of expressions of apology, they like to give money, food or some useful gift to those whose feelings they have hurt. But aren't tangible gestures and acts just as meaningless if they aren't done with a genuine heart?

The Akkosa Sutta records a thought-provoking incident in the life of the Buddha. On one occasion, when the Buddha was walking past a village, a furious young man approached him. This stranger started hurling insults at the sage and using foul language to give vent to his hatred.

"When you have visitors, don't you offer them things to eat?" asked the Buddha.

"Yes, I do," replied the man.

"But, if the visitors refuse to accept what is given, to whom does the food then belong?" asked the Teacher.

"To me," answered the man.

"Similarly, all the abuse that you have just said belongs to you for I don't accept it," remarked the Buddha.

In the course of giving a short sermon, the Master declared: "Where is anger for one who has transcended it? The person who repays anger with anger is worse than the angry man." The spirit of what he taught is that it is via forgiveness and never resorting to retaliation that one finds the supreme peace.

One of the few outstanding Hindu saints of our time was Swami Ramdas (1884-1963). When he was a schoolboy, he often played truant and distanced himself from school and from arithmetic, which was his pet aversion. His spirit yearned for freedom. Naturally, from his teachers he received the most cruel chastisement, but he loved them nevertheless.

Let us briefly look at the question of forgiveness from the standpoint of Christian theology. Does man really have the power to forgive another person in the sense of pardoning his sins? One would have thought that only God alone has the power to do that, assuming, of course, the existence of an Omnipresent, Omnipotent, and Omniscient Supreme Being.

What did Jesus say at the time of his crucifixion? He never said, as many believe, "I forgive them." His real words were: "Father, forgive them for they know not what they do." We can conclude from this final declaration of Jesus that he was only a mere vehicle of the Divine and not the Divine per se. It implies that Christian worship should be directed not to Jesus, but to the Father.

We can also examine this issue from the karmic vantage point. We all have to face the consequences of our past thoughts and deeds at some time or other. In short, we reap what we have sown. My lot in life is determined entirely by my past karma. The joys and sorrows that I experience in this life can be traced back to my karma, to my good and bad deeds respectively. So, extending that logic, when a man inflicts upon me a serious injury, I cannot blame him for my physical and mental suffering. I can only blame *myself* and my past bad karma for it. Therefore, it is pointless for the man to ask me for forgiveness (if at all he ever does). And regarding the man's role in what has taken place, he was simply instrumental in executing the karmic law.

When a compassionate person, aware of the operations of karmic law, is robbed or attacked, he neither expects the offender to suffer from pangs of regret later nor does he hope that the wrongdoer will ever ask for his forgiveness. He merely tries to understand the psychological causes of the malefactor's crimes and leaves it at that. This is precisely what I did when I was attacked by a gang of skinheads while I was going for a walk once in London. They hit me on my head with a beer bottle. I bled profusely and I was rushed to a hospital. I can truthfully state that I have never harboured any resentment against these white supremacists. I only found myself being more careful when strolling along the roads after this incident. I never expected those misguided youngsters to trace my whereabouts to ask for forgiveness. Never. I tried only to understand the workings of the criminal and violent mind and left it at that.

This incident marks an important turning point in my life for then and there I decided to leave England for good. I did so with considerable sadness for I was attached to London. Before long, I moved to Australia after finding a job there. Although I had forgiven the British racists, I still feel scared even to make a brief visit to their country. So, in a way, I have not completely forgiven them.

SOCIAL ACTIVITIES
FROM A SPIRITUAL
POINT OF VIEW

6
SOCIAL ACTIVITIES FROM A SPIRITUAL POINT OF VIEW

I have been invited to give a public talk on the interesting subject of social activities from a spiritual point of view. I am indeed happy to accept this invitation and to be here with you today.

When a group of people gather together to explore otherworldly matters in a spirit of friendliness and brotherhood, that, in itself, is a spiritual activity. Unfortunately, in some parts of the world today, there is religious intolerance. There are countries where only one religion is acceptable to the government. And then, there are nations like France where the policy of the state is to be indifferent to religion. There is a strict separation between state and church. It is called *laïcité* in which religion is kept out of the educational system in state schools. One of the inevitable consequences of this policy is a general lack of interest in the fascinating field of comparative religion. Though many people in the country celebrate Christmas and there is a lot of drinking and merry-making, rarely in their social activities do they discuss the saintly life of Jesus and his ethical teachings. Ethical values are no longer taken seriously, with the result that children are often unable to distinguish between right and wrong. Sick and elderly parents are often not well looked after by their ungrateful children. Telling lies was once a sin but now it has become a fine art.

Religious persons sometimes like to give public expression to their religious beliefs by participating in street processions. Such outward demonstrations of faith are disallowed in some countries. Is that a loss? Dictatorial governments can imprison you because they dislike your views or beliefs. But can any government actually control the inner operations of your heart and mind? Politicians in powerful positions can only influence you, but can they ever restrain you from what you like to think or believe? A prisoner, for example, is free to practise his religion or engage in meditation in the privacy of his prison cell. Meditation, in fact, is best done when one is alone in a quiet room, undisturbed by the presence of anyone else. But some extroverted individuals like to show off their religiosity by meditating, chanting, and praying in public! They then run the risk of stirring up the anger of repressive governments and intolerant individuals.

An Indian guru was sitting next to a communist while they were travelling in an aeroplane.

"Man cannot live by bread alone," thundered the bearded guru.

"Yes, of course," remarked the communist. "Man needs butter and jam to go with the bread."

This funny incident highlights the wall of misunderstanding that separates worldly people from the otherworldly. Mundane men and women are mostly concerned with the problems of ordinary life such as trying to eke out an existence in a world in which jobs are becoming increasingly difficult to find. But those with spiritual values do not give much importance to bread and butter questions, for they are keen on leading simple lives that are morally correct. This they can do with a modest income and because their needs are fewer, they have far less burdens to carry in life. The world, alas, is becoming more and more secular. The day might come when no public or outer expressions of one's religious affiliations are allowed. We might have to settle for a situation where religion is regarded solely as a private matter. Even so, can we not express our spirituality by means of various social activities? In the course of this talk, I shall describe several ways of doing this.

In my life, perhaps the most important social activity has been the writing and publishing of books on various subjects. A good many of these published writings have been on spiritual unfolding and comparative religion. My books are freely distributed to anyone interested in reading them and also to universities and other academic, national, and public libraries. It is my intention to continue this work until the end of my days. I regret that the demand for books in Europe is diminishing whereas it is fast increasing in Asia,

Africa, and the Far East. Why, I wonder, is the reading habit slowly disappearing in some parts of the world? Many people prefer computers and television to reading serious books. At present, there is an attitude of indifference to spiritual subjects in Europe. It's just a sad sign of the times that the vast majority of people are extremely sceptical about what religions have to offer. Their lack of faith in the beliefs of their forefathers is exerting a powerful influence over the minds of their children and grandchildren.

Another important social activity of mine is helping the helpless and the poverty-stricken. There are hundreds of homeless and penniless refugees in the city of Marseille who have to live on the insufficient handouts of the state. A good portion of these needy people are refugees from countries torn apart by the stupid wars that have been waged in Europe and elsewhere. About twice a month, Claudia and I visit Marseille for the purpose of distributing free food, clothes, and books amongst these extremely poor people. Because they had to flee to France in a hurry from their war-torn native lands, some of them are still traumatised and mentally unstable.

What is our attitude towards these folk? We don't look down upon them by treating them as inferiors, scroungers, social parasites or illegal immigrants. We treat them as equals who are now in reduced circumstances, largely due to the folly of our warmongering politicians. We never blame these unfortunate refugees for their problems. They are the victims of our human hate. It is our hate—yes, our collective hate—that manifests itself in the form of war. Therefore, isn't it our individual responsibility to meditate, turning our attention inwards, and thereby eliminate every trace of hate within ourselves? Every visit to Marseille reminds us of our spiritual responsibility to devote some time each day to meditation. Meditation is the path to inner purity.

In one famous passage of the *Bhagavad Gita*, Lord Krishna advises Arjuna that actions must be done without any desire for the fruits, advantages or benefits resulting from those actions. One of the greatest messages of the *Bhagavad Gita* is the importance of *Nishkama Karma* or unmotivated action. Actions, in other words, should have no ulterior motive whatsoever. *Nishkama Karma* consists in simply working for its own sake. Our charitable donations, therefore, are made without expecting love, gratitude, appreciation or admiration from others.

"What a fine gesture!" remarked a passerby who saw me giving some sandwiches to a beggar. I ignored the compliment and continued working.

Once, we gave bread and fruits to a Muslim lady who was squatting on the pavement. She smiled, showing us how happy she was to receive this simple offering.

"Allah is noting down all the good things you're doing," she said, lifting her veil. "Allah is surely reserving for you a special place in Paradise."

"Allah is kind," I replied. "But I'm not particularly interested in going to Paradise." I forgot to tell her that doing something to alleviate poverty with all its attendant suffering is my idea of paradise.

There is a widespread view that many beggars are lazy and rather reluctant to work. There is an element of truth in that. But we frequently fail to see that it's not at all easy to beg. Those who are swelled with pride can't bring themselves to beg. One of the things we can learn from beggars, monks, nuns, and *sannyasis* is humility.

But there is a vast difference between humility and being without an ego. It is relatively easy for a wandering mendicant to live a life without possessions. I know from first-hand experience of working with sannyasis that some of them don't have even a suitcase to carry their few personal effects. But nearly all the sannyasis I have known did possess an ego. Often, the ego is invisible and exists in a subtle form.

I have mentioned the fact that sannyasis have a minimum of possessions and also that they are humble people. But they are extremely attached to their egos. High is their sense of self-esteem. Their strong attachment to their egos is evidence of their spiritual pride! I am reminded of a saying by Sri Ramakrishna Paramahamsa on this subject. Sri Ramakrishna, quoting Bibhishana, remarked that the vanity of a saint regarding his sainthood is hard indeed to drop. The greatest sannyasi is the one who has gone beyond the ego and dropped it once and for all. In the history of religion, the Buddha stands out for he succeeded in cleansing himself of each and every trace of egotism.

I must confess that there are times when I'm not one hundred per cent selfless when making charitable donations, especially when I take part in alms-givings, in which there is a selfish motive. Following the funeral of a relation or friend, Buddhists have alms-givings. *Bhikkhus* are invited to homes for lavish lunches. On such special occasions, Buddhists are generous in their practice of giving alms. The merit accruing from such deeds is transferred to the dear departed ones. There is an element of selfishness in giving merit *only* to those who were once dear and near to us, whereas a selfless person would transfer the merit to *each and every* deceased human being. In addition, donations are usually made to accumulate merit for *oneself* also.

A person with a scientific bent of mind once asked me to prove that merit actually gets transferred. I had to tell him that this religious practice has no scientific basis. In fact, many of our religious customs have no scientific support. Yet, we do certain things out of intense devotion. Isn't that good enough a reason for what we do? Besides, during their lifetimes, our parents instilled in us the importance of having regular alms-givings in memory of them once they would be no more. So, we have alms-givings not only to transfer merit, but also in honour of them since they raised us.

In all our social activities, such as when having conversations with friends or strangers, we shouldn't say anything in support of war. Never being a party to the injuring or killing of animals or human beings is one of the essential requirements of spirituality. Mahatma Gandhi, the great apostle of *Ahimsa* or non-violence, urged us to throw away the gun and practise loving-kindness in thought, word, and deed. Spiritual men and women are naturally opposed to all forms of bloodshed. Alas, the economies of some countries depend heavily on the production and sale of armaments. What a shame!

Harming anyone, even the worst enemy, is horrible. How cruel and barbaric to shoot at animals or human beings! Thousands of years ago we were hunter-gatherers. Something of that animalism still remains dormant in our unconscious mind. That is why we enjoy blood sports and relish the taste of meat, fish, and the like.

Under no circumstances will I ever justify the violence perpetrated by the state. I am naturally against the existence of armies, navies, and air forces in the world. Since the state is committed to militarism, it seems to me that the only way to ensure peace and harmony in the world is to abolish all armies, navies, and air forces. Someday, when human beings become really civilised, there will surely arise a stateless world in which national frontiers will be seen as a thing of the past. When there is total disarmament, all the money we are wasting on our useless and silly wars today can be diverted to the economic, social, cultural, and spiritual betterment of our planet.

In my social life, whenever possible, I have always preached pacifism. Pacifists strongly disapprove of violence and war. We maintain that differences of opinion can be amicably settled via discussion and compromise without recourse to fighting. If we seriously want a world in which we can all live happily and peacefully, instead of leading lives filled with fear and insecurity, it is absolutely necessary for all of us to become pacifists.

Do you remember the experience of falling in love for the first time in your life? What happens when a young boy and a young girl grow very fond of each other? In their pure innocence, they don't give a damn about each other's social class, caste, colour, race, religion or nationality. When you love someone with all your heart and soul, all feelings of division suddenly disappear. Doesn't the behaviour of the youthful couple send us an important message? The lesson we can learn is this: love and love alone is the determining factor in the removal of national, social, racial, and religious barriers. Whenever there is genuine affection, it becomes possible to go beyond all the man-made obstacles to living and working together in harmony.

Although I am giving a talk on social activities, the truth of the matter is that my wife and I are involved in very few social activities in which there is a lot of interaction with other people. We are more like two hermits who live in the same house, having little contact with the outside world. Because we are strict vegetarians who neither drink nor smoke, seldom do we receive invitations to birthday parties, weddings and other such social occasions. That isn't a great deprivation. Who likes to go to functions in which one cannot avoid tobacco fumes and the stench of cooked chicken, fish or meat? Those who partake in such social events are indirectly encouraging the consumption of fish, flesh, and fowl. Not only that, they also become a party to the actions of the animal killing industry. In situations of this kind, they probably acquire some bad karma.

We do not openly propagate vegetarianism. We do so indirectly. When we open our doors to guests, they soon discover that it is possible to lead a healthy and ethically correct life by not eating meat, fish or chicken. Despite the fact that some guests are somewhat saddened to find that ours is a house without wine, they soon realise that one can be truly happy and cheerful without becoming enslaved by the bottle.

Only rarely do we have guests who are profoundly interested in spiritual development. For that supreme purpose, the spiritually-inclined already know the importance of being able to think clearly. Therefore, we never have to remind them of the danger of taking alcohol or hallucinogenic drugs. Anything that distorts perception, needless to say, stands in the way of clarity.

Occasionally, there are visitors in search of yogic knowledge. They usually want to find if there are yogic cures for their minor ailments. We show them yogic postures and breathing techniques that are relevant to their problems. We tell them that these yogic exercises, if regularly practised, might soon put an end to their troubles.

According to Patanjali, *Asana* and *Pranayama* are only the second and third rungs respectively of his eightfold ladder leading to *Samadhi*, which is the eighth or final rung. *Samadhi* is the summit or pinnacle of yogic achievement.

Newcomers to yoga need to be told that yoga is a way of life. Yoga is a preparation for spiritual liberation. For this reason, they should neither regard it merely as a means of treating illnesses nor see it only as a method of beautifying the body. In the same way, neither should they view yoga solely as a system of relaxation nor must they see it just as a wonderful antidote to stress. Without craving for any of the benefits of yoga, they can simply practise yoga for its own sake. The clear-sighted can't help practising yoga because they are already yogis with their heads turned towards the Eternal.

What then is yoga? After a lifetime of doing yoga, I can get into postures naturally and without strain. Yoga makes my body supple and relaxed; the body becomes ready for effortless meditation. Meditation, I know, will enable me to discover my defilements and thereby, transcend all of them forever. If I manage to go thus far, it would be possible to go beyond the intellect and enter that celestial sphere called *Samadhi*.

Ladies and gentlemen, I want to say one last thing in conclusion: We all sincerely feel the need to create a flawless social order. But an ideal society can never arise so long as the individuals living in society continue to think, feel, and behave like savages. Therefore, it seems to me that what is absolutely necessary is for each one of us to clear up the mess within ourselves. This cannot be done through the pressure of governments and strict laws. Society cannot be changed by acts of parliament. Man has to purify himself individually. Hence the immense importance of spirituality. If we succeed in becoming spiritually transformed, then we will be automatically laying the foundation for the creation of a perfect society.

An address to the Siva Nandi Foundation in Zürich
(Switzerland) on May 24th 2015

7

JOY OF GIVING

Some of the happiest people I have met were full of generosity. Giving practical expression to this noble quality came naturally to them. But, I have also known men and women who were so stingy that the act of giving even a few coins in charity was a painful and unpleasant loss for them. In nearly every society, one can find munificent men and women as well as mean mortals at the other end of the spectrum. "To which of these categories do I belong?" is a question that has to be answered sooner or later by every soul-searching seeker.

Children seem to know instinctively the answer to this question. They quickly differentiate between the loving aunt who showers them with presents and the indifferent and aloof uncle who does not. While they become fond of the former, they begin to loathe the latter. This is because kids, like adults, are driven solely by self-interest. In this respect, are grown-ups any different from their children?

I have sometimes heard it said that a new-born baby has a *tabula rasa*. They are supposed to bring with them unblemished minds that are innocent and ready to record impressions as though for the first time. If they were that pure, there would not be in them any trace of selfishness. Since that is not the case, can we not reasonably assume that the minds of infants are already conditioned at the time of birth? During incalculable periods of time covering thousands and thousands of previous births, selfish tendencies in the form of an ego, an 'I' or a 'me' did emerge again and again. Although we cannot trace the ego's origins, we can be sure that it exists and is quite active in the mind of every child.

I believe that I have a right to give away only those things that legally belong to me. For the sake of investigating this question, we can ignore my legal rights for the moment. But does anything really belong to me? For example, I possess my furniture and use it daily, but philosophically and ethically speaking, do I own it? I can make good use of it only for the duration of my life, not for all eternity. This means that I am no more than the temporary user and possessor of it, for I am not going to live forever. I am more like a leaser than an owner. As I can never be its owner for all time, the furniture is not really mine. What I have already stated about my furniture is equally applicable to everything else I am supposed to own and possess legally. In all truth, I do *not* own anything. Understanding this simple but profound principle results in the sudden advent of a new attitude to everything one had hitherto regarded as one's own—a sense of non-attachment. The moment this sense of non-attachment begins to permeate our minds and hearts, it becomes considerably easier to part with all the things we own. The spirit of generosity towards all living beings comes easily when our bonds of attachment break. Then the process of giving provisions to the needy, free of charge, of course, happens naturally; it takes place without a struggle.

Several times in my previous publications, I have written at length about our practice of distributing bread and fruits to refugees, dropouts, beggars, and homeless people who line the pavements of Marseille, doing so approximately once a fortnight throughout the year, except during the cold wintry period. For Claudia and I who hand out the food alone, this somewhat arduous work is a labour of love. But what we do is just a drop in the ocean of charitable work, for immeasurably vast is the problem of poverty in the world. I refer to this matter in passing while writing on the need to give because if more and more people start serving those living on the breadline, I am sure that all such deeds might at least alleviate the problem, even if they do not solve it altogether. Doing something is better than doing nothing. And the cheerful smiles of those who receive the food show us that they are truly appreciative of what we do. Who does not like the feeling of being cared for and looked after?

Why is it that we have become so profit-oriented? Why do we seize every available opportunity to make a quick buck? Is anything ever done out of the sheer goodness of our hearts? It is a sign of the times that so few of our activities spring from affection. Rarely are our services rendered without a price tag attached to them. Seldom do we give anything away for nothing. Yet, there are exceptions, like the community I live in, where the residents like to give away whatever they do not need to thrift shops or charities. These organisations are so efficient that they can quickly distribute aid to victims of floods, earthquakes, and other natural catastrophes. Many donate not only their old clothes, but also new ones for victims of disasters. Sometimes we have given even objets d'art to antique shops for the poor sellers to augment their income.

I reckon that we have donated thousands of copies of our published books to the national, university, and special libraries of different nations. During the last forty years, we have been very busy doing this thankless work, not that we are fishing for compliments. We hope that these libraries will make these works available to the future generations so that they who take the trouble to read them can broaden their horizons.

Once, I was trying to answer a question posed by a London cabbie while he was taking me for a long drive through the city. He asked me what I did during my spare time and I replied that during my spare time I wrote books that were donated thereafter to libraries. He could not, for the life of him, understand why I distributed my books free of charge. He thought it ridiculous that I voluntarily put myself in a situation from which I failed to benefit financially.

"Chum," he said, "tell me what's in it for you?"

"There's no monetary gain whatsoever," I explained. "On the one hand, there's nothing, but on the other hand the sense of fulfilment that comes makes me feel that all the time and energy spent on the writing and production of the book was worthwhile. Readers will begin to know about its existence with the passage of time. Who knows, however, whether in the distant future the title is going to be relegated to the dustbin or treated as an immortal classic? But I think that most books remain in limbo for all eternity. What a fate!"

The United States and several wealthy European nations have been and still are in the practice of giving vast sums of money to impoverished Third World economies. For a period of a few years, I worked for the Ministry of Overseas Development that would provide money and technical knowhow to poor Asian and African countries. The poverty-stricken nations that receive such aid, beyond doubt, have benefited tremendously from it. But, more often than not, the assistance comes with strings attached! For example, the recipients of such largesse would be persuaded or pressurised to use at least part of the money they receive to purchase the products of the donor countries; then out of feelings of deep gratitude, the underdeveloped country would do so. Later they feel trapped. Once an economically weaker African or Asian state accepts freely-given agricultural machinery from a prosperous country and then begins to use that equipment, what usually happens? Impressed by the efficiency and high speed of the new appliances, the farmers will soon find them indispensable because of their efficiency. Before long, the poor country starts placing orders for the purchase of this very same machinery! It is an open secret that this kind of so-called foreign aid is a subtle form of good long-term investment. Instead of acting in the above-mentioned manner which, though it cannot be called a dishonest one by any means, seems somewhat devious, would it not be better if these needy people were treated not as mere instruments for self-enrichment, but as free individuals in their own right who deserve to be helped for their *own sake*? Ulterior motives besmirch the donors' otherwise good and generous deeds.

Even in democracies, it is extremely difficult for private individuals to influence the thinking of those in positions of power, those who make the important political and economic decisions. Are politicians always ethically inspired? Isn't it rare that their actions are stimulated by lofty ideals? Can they be trusted to think and act altruistically?

Is it possible to change the hearts and minds of people by means of legislation? By passing acts of parliament, only superficial changes can be brought about in society. For example, one can reduce the level of petroleum pollution by strictly ensuring that in cities only certain prescribed kinds of non-toxic fuel should be used. But no law can effectively change either human nature in general or man's selfishness in particular.

The religious teachers and prophets of yore have decreed that we should not kill, steal, tell lies, sexually misbehave and so forth. Their exhortations to become *humane* human beings have been ignored by the masses; the saintly few who heeded them were, to some degree, spiritually metamorphosed. This great internal transformation is not something that lends itself to being handed over to those who are shrouded in the mist of *samsara*. How many people are actually keen on self-exploration and self-purification that results in the transcendence of selfishness? It goes without saying that altruism, in its purest form, exists only when selfishness drops.

Since genuine generosity comes only when one is impelled by altruism, it is obviously necessary to understand the latter. Altruism is the undeviating devotion to the interests of others as opposed to one's own private interests. Let us, therefore, explore this subject of altruism in depth by illustrating a few instances that show either the absence or presence of altruism.

A doctor would be acting altruistically when he does his very best to cure a patient who is suffering from chronic asthma. He works very hard. After several months, he notices that his patient has begun to recover. Needless to say, both the medical practitioner and the patient are happy on seeing the first signs of improvement. Impressed by the patient's rapid progress, the doctor forecasts that the complete cure of the patient is likely to happen very soon. Yet, he also realises that someday in the near future, when the convalescent gets completely cured, the latter would cease to be one of his patients. Consequently, there will be a decline in the doctor's income. This realisation would coincide with a corresponding decline in the eager doctor's motivation to hasten the patient's recovery. What transpires at the moment the doctor realises that his services would shortly come to an end? "I'll soon lose a patient and that will be a loss." What a shame that his cold and calculating nature and his selfishness, in other words, suddenly eclipse the doctor's initial altruism!

Would loving doctors who are more interested in the good health of the ailing in their charge than in the size of their bank balances ever have a conflict of interests between their patients and their bank balances? Those who serve others and those who offer presents are in the same category, in the sense that both groups must *never* soil their hands with the dirty waters of selfishness.

Why, I wonder, do doctors get scared of the possibility of a fall in their earnings? Do they not make enough money already? Have you ever met a poor doctor? In all my travels, I have never come across a single penniless physician. In the past, there were exemplary medical practitioners like Dr. Albert Schweitzer, a master musician and missionary, who served humanity without asking anything in return. Did Jesus charge anything when he healed the sick and the possessed?

Dear reader, have you ever heard the story of the unemployed university graduate in rags? The poor man has a chance encounter on the road with a banker in a dark three-piece suit.

"Please give me some money," begs the hungry man.

"Today, I haven't any spare coins," says the banker.

"In that case, you can pay me by cheque or bank notes," replies the tramp.

This discussion has regretfully become somewhat theoretical. Therefore, it is time to write about how my wife and I try to give practical expression to what we think is our altruism. We are not perfect human beings. We are not yet fully enlightened. So, while bearing in mind the importance of being indifferent to the fruits of our actions, which is one of the main messages of the *Bhagavad Gita*, we avoid acting egoistically whenever we are engaged in giving.

As we take pleasure in organic gardening, a good portion of our large garden is used to grow vegetables and fruits. The vegetables from the land are never enough for all our needs, although we are only two people who exist on a vegetarian diet. But whenever we find an abundance of fruits, be they cherries, figs or persimmons (kaki), we hand out the surplus. Almost always there are more fruits than what we require. The profit-orientated folk would like to sell the excess, particularly if they are in dire financial straits, which is understandable. Owing to our rather austere lifestyle, there are no great difficulties in balancing the budget. Every year we give away freely a fair amount of fruits to neighbours, friends, passers-by, and total strangers we meet in the streets.

How do the recipients of these gifts react? Only a handful have the desire to give verbal expressions of thanks; they accept what is offered with a warm smile. That is fair enough. A good many accept the products of our garden with a certain embarrassment. They probably feel truly grateful, but at the same time, also experience a sense of deep frustration because of their inability to reciprocate the gesture, for whatever reason. The cynics, however, stare at us in stunned silence, somewhat puzzled at our gesture of goodwill, wondering what ulterior motives lie hidden behind our conduct. Since one of my pastimes is thought-reading—some strongly disapprove of it—I have recorded the following findings of mine in this regard.

"This foreign fellow and his Anglophone woman are doing all this to endear themselves to us!" thinks a potbellied, middle-aged local when we give him a plastic bagful of cherries.

We picked some newly ripened figs from our garden and handed them to a priest. Frocked in a long white cassock, the tall and stately man slowly bows low in a thankful gesture. "They aren't bad people, although they don't go to church," he thinks while saying goodbye.

While walking past the house of a neighbour, I notice that he is busy mowing his lawn, it being a lovely morning in the autumn. After exchanging greetings, I offer him some of our oversupply of garden produce—a dozen delicious persimmons that are very ripe and gold in colour.

"I simply adore them," he remarks while accepting the offer. The next moment he thinks, "This man wants to be friendly with me so that I'll vote for him when someday he stands for election to the local council."

Once, a Moroccan friend of ours returned to France from his annual holiday in Casablanca, his home town, bringing with him heaps of Moroccan sweets and cakes of various kinds and gave us a substantial portion of it. However, neither Claudia nor I have a strong liking for sugary foods. Faced with the problem of giving away Moroccan confectionery, I knocked at the door of a casual acquaintance, a garage mechanic with several children. The man opened the door and accepted the large plateful of sweets.

"*Merci, merci*," he said, showing his appreciation and accepting the sweets.

After he closed the door, I had to stay there for a few minutes to tie my shoelaces. It was then that I overheard him telling his wife about my visit.

"Darling," he said in a loud voice. "That do-gooder, religious nut has brought something to eat!"

We are glad whenever we have the opportunity to give food to a hungry human being. But we are happiest when feeding animals. Claudia feeds cats, dogs, and other stray animals, especially the abandoned ones that she finds in the course of our wanderings through crowded cities and the open countryside. Unlike the animals that we feed, when a group of people is treated to a sumptuous feast, you will find at least one or two inveterate grumblers who will complain about the poor quality of a dish that was on the table. There is nothing that they enjoy more than kicking up a fuss. Such is the way that human beings behave. Now, when it comes to how animals behave when they are fed, they neither talk back to you nor talk about you behind your back. Birds, for instance, are good guests who never overstay. Once they have eaten, they like to fly away. The tiny sparrows that chirp, the ashen pigeons that coo, and the black and white magpies that screech are the noisiest of the birds that frequent us. They visit the garden, perch on top of the tall dark green cypresses, devour their favourite foods from the ground, and eat the grains that Claudia affectionately gives them. They eat only to satisfy their hunger. The event is soon forgotten both by us who offer the food and they who consume it. The birds do not express their thanks, nor do we ever expect them to do so. What a beautiful relationship between birds and humans! How I wish it were possible for human beings to have between themselves such harmony! Why have we become so complicated? Birds, like celestial beings, can fly; that is a faculty that we lack, which shows that birds are in some ways more skilful than us. Besides, these feathered friends have a lightness, quickness, and simplicity which is so sadly wanting in earthbound two-legged creatures like us who are so proud about our supposed superiority.

Until now we have considered only the giving away of material things. Let us discuss non-material items such as knowledge, information, ideas and the like that can also be offered to people. Although these are invisible to the naked eye, they can be understood by the mind. Strictly speaking, they are, like thought, a form of matter that is incorporeal and intangible. Be that as it may, we can revert to the question of sharing with others everything that we know. On account of her education and wide reading, my wife is knowledgeable about several subjects, particularly nutrition and good health. She unstintingly passes on the useful and practical information that she has gathered to persons with minor ailments. The unsolicited advice is sometimes rejected, but those who accept it and take immediate action often reap the benefits.

Why do we feel proprietorial about the knowledge that we have acquired during our long courses of study leading to university degrees? Why take pride in our academic achievements? Anyone with the same motivation can follow the same courses and get the same qualifications! Knowledge is common property, in the sense that it is neither yours nor mine, which means that every person should have free access to it. Without the slightest bit of hesitation, we have to be ready to transmit to others, for the sake of their welfare and happiness, the things we have laboriously learned. For just like material things, we cannot take away with us our learning when it is time to depart this life.

Generosity is generally regarded as a virtue. But for the person who is truly generous, the acts of giving and sharing are things that happen spontaneously, effortlessly, and unintentionally, like breathing in and breathing out all the time. The open-handed ones are often quite unconscious of the fact that they are overflowing with the spirit of giving and sharing, it all being part and parcel of their inner nature.

8
NEGATE
NARROW
NATIONALISM

What a shame that even after living in France for more than two decades, I still can't speak French fluently, let alone write with elegance in this noble language! Many are the reasons that I can give for this sad situation, but I realise that in the end, I have only myself to blame for it.

My knowledge of French is rather basic. Although I can make myself understood when I visit a police station, railway station, post office, bank or supermarket, often I fail to grasp fully what others say in reply to my questions. I can follow only about fifty per cent of what is being said in French. It might seem like a minor miracle that with such an inadequate comprehension of the language, I still succeeded in surviving in France for all these years. But, that was not at all mind-boggling because my wife, Claudia, was usually by my side when we were in public. She knows French, English, and German (her mother tongue) pretty well. I shudder to think what will happen when there is no good interpreter. Through signs will I have to communicate? What a frightening possibility!

Claudia was born and bred in Switzerland where French is one of the several official languages. Like fresh cream that blends in perfectly with Swiss chocolates, she had no difficulty whatsoever in mixing well with the locals and becoming an integral part of French society. Despite my low levels of proficiency in French, I am happy to state that I do have a few French-born friends. It is noteworthy that whenever emotional bonds between friends get forged, language barriers fade into insignificance.

I regret that my French is of poor quality because it means that in France, I am unable to carry on a serious conversation for long; I do not know how to compose an article, nor do I have the capacity to draw up a petition. I had to say no on the two or three occasions when people asked me to give public lectures in French. Whenever I had to turn down such invitations, I felt a sense of frustration, especially because I was quite experienced in giving public talks in English. Will I ever master French? So far, all my efforts to learn the language thoroughly have been in vain. After years of hard work and endless struggles, I am still like a raw beginner.

Please let me narrate the story of my short-lived flirtations with the French language over the years. Dear reader, I do so not so much to get your sympathy for the terrible troubles I've had while studying the language as to understand the problems facing *all* learners of French, who do *not* come from the francophone world of an estimated 220 million French speakers.

In 1956, I was a student in Colombo. I can still remember the mass demonstrations in the streets against the Franco-British military involvement in Egypt during the Suez crisis. President Nasser's nationalisation of the Suez Canal greatly displeased some countries in the West and upset most countries in the East. During that epoch, the foreign policies of both Britain and France were regarded with a certain degree of suspicion by Asian people. I saw demonstrators shouting hostile slogans outside the British and French embassies in Colombo. Although I did not actively participate in these demonstrations against the former colonial powers, my heart went out to those angry men and women who were voicing the aspirations of the newly emergent nations of Asia and Africa. However, my antipathy towards France soon disappeared, especially after reading the entertaining short stories of Guy de Maupassant and enjoying French films such as *Et Dieu créa la femme* in which Brigitte Bardot featured prominently. I particularly liked all the films in which Maurice Chevalier acted and sang. I don't think I'll ever forget the catchy French words and phrases that I picked up while watching these movies: "*Paris sera toujours Paris*" and "*Ça sent si bon la France*". I began learning French with smiles, not with tears as some do.

Yet, when I recall all the missed opportunities in my life, which I do sometimes, tears do well up in my eyes. Why did I fail to make hay while the tropical sun was shining in all its glory? Foremost among these lost chances was my failure to follow a course in French at the Alliance Française de

Colombo, where my late teens had been spent. At that time, I met many who had benefited from their courses, with the result that they could speak and write French reasonably well. The students of the Alliance Française were drawn from ordinary schools and the higher echelons of the state bureaucracy. They all had a good word for the Alliance Française de Colombo.

What was it that prevented me from going there? Schoolwork, homework, and extracurricular activities such as leisure reading were all time-consuming. Yet, during that period, had I been able to foretell that a good portion of my life was going to be spent in France, I would have squeezed a French course into my busy life, no matter the difficulty. In retrospect, I should have done just that. My capacity to absorb the French language would have been far easier then, when I was a youngster with a more impressionable mind, as against now, when I am a retiree with a mind that has gotten clogged up with millions of memories and information of doubtful value. By writing in this vein, am I not trying to find an excuse for not working hard on my French?

My first lesson in French was in my late teens at St Joseph's College in Trichinopoly, which is situated in the arid, searing heat of south India. Trichy is a bustling, dusty, noisy town close to the Cauvery River, which is sacred to the Hindus.

Run by Jesuits, St Joseph's College was famous for its high academic standards. A fair number of teachers were Jesuit priests dressed in long white cassocks with red sashes around their waists. These grave and strictly celibate European and Indian priests followed a set of rigid rules and behaved like a regiment of extremely disciplined soldiers. Although the Jesuit teachers were passionately dedicated to learning, I felt that they, in their religious and missionary zeal, were stifling the natural curiosity of young and innocent students. Their freedom to think was circumscribed by an inflexible set of religious beliefs and dogmas. Deep down in my gut, I already knew that education was more than the mere gathering of knowledge: it was the process of inquiring into all and everything, with an open mind. But I found, much to my dismay, that rational research into philosophical questions in general, and religious issues in particular, were frowned upon by the teaching staff. I should have known better before I joined the college that Jesuits were not so much thinkers as believers. Utterly disillusioned with this institution, I left it after staying in Trichy for a short period of only two terms.

I never knew the name of the French teacher at St Joseph's College. All his pupils and the staff addressed him as "French Father". A thin, tall, blond priest with deep blue eyes and an angular face, French Father was probably the most popular teacher in the college. He was well liked because if students were late for class or forgot to do their homework, French Father would never pull them up or give a scolding.

"I'm not here to punish you," he would say. "I leave

that job to the Almighty. If you don't study, you're first of all answerable to Him and then to your parents."

There was another reason why this teacher was so popular. Each French class would last for one hour, but he taught only for about fifteen or twenty minutes at the most; the rest of the time was spent by French Father talking on subjects such as interesting places to visit in France, politics, and sports.

There were only about twelve students in the French class, and a good portion of them consisted of Brahmin boys who dressed in the traditional manner. They would wear hand spun, hand-woven white cloths wrapped around their slim waists. The frontal parts of their heads were shaved, giving them the appearance of having large foreheads. Their uncut long hair was tied in a bun. Highly amused by their hairstyle, French Father would regard them as females, although all the students in the college were male.

"Will the girl in the back row answer this question?" French Father would say with a smile. Whenever he referred to a student as a girl, French Father was making fun of Hindu practices. I felt on those occasions that this Christian clergyman was subtly trying to undermine the religious faith of the Hindu schoolboys.

French Father drilled into us the importance of having a thorough understanding of how to use the auxiliary verbs 'être' and 'avoir', as well as the modal verbs 'vouloir', 'pouvoir', 'devoir' and 'savoir'. We also had to memorise and learn how certain irregular verbs had to be conjugated. It was by no means easy.

Of the several different activities involved in the learning of French, such as knowing the rules of grammar and pronunciation, the memorisation of new words to increase our vocabulary was, by far, the most interesting. French Father, notwithstanding the fact that he was a full-blooded Frenchman who was proud of his origins, approached the problem in the age-old Indian manner of reciting aloud a mantra. Each student in the class had to stand up and repeat twelve times the new word he had just learned. For example, we went through the ritual of reciting, *"Peut-être* means perhaps". Soul-destroying repetitious work of this kind was tedious, trying, and tiring.

"Why twelve?" a Brahmin boy once dared to ask.

"In remembrance of the twelve apostles," answered French Father with his azure eyes turned upwards with reverence.

The Brahmin boys always stood out in the class because of their retentive memory. They had to hear a new word only once and it would be glued to their minds forever. There is a consensus among Indians that Brahmins have minds with exceptionally developed retentive capacities. For centuries, their ancestors used to memorise the Vedas and various sacred texts. People are impressed when Brahmins rattle off the scriptures, but whether they can also correctly understand the ancient verses or not is quite another matter.

Today, nearly six decades later, I don't have to rack my brains when learning new words. I have devised my own method for making a new word stick in my mind. First, I will look the unfamiliar word up in an etymological dictionary and get some information about its derivation. And then, I will close my eyes for a minute or two and try to incorporate the new word in a sentence.

The rote learning of history, especially the history of classical times, prevailed in this college. The majority of students found the study of ancient history rather boring, but it was a compulsory subject so it couldn't be avoided. Matters were made worse because a good many chapters in our ancient history textbook were simply incomprehensible.

"Never mind if you can't understand the book," advised the teacher of this subject who had a down-to-earth approach towards his professorial job. "You just learn by heart the sections you don't understand. Always in the exam paper, there's a question on the causes of the Peloponnesian War. Memorise the relevant lines. At least you can show off your powers of recall and get good marks to pass the exam."

In the French class, there were two clever Brahmin boys whose names I can still remember—Mahadevan and Gopal. Both were similar insofar as they were very studious and cheeky. Mahadevan had the habit of addressing the priest in a casual way.

"Have you done your homework?" French Father once demanded.

"Yes sir," replied Mahadevan.

"You keep on calling me 'sir', but I'm not a bank manager," complained French Father. "You should call me 'Father'."

"If I call you 'Father', I'll be insulting my mother!" retorted Mahadevan.

Whenever French Father referred to God, he had the habit of looking in an upward direction. One day, the clergyman was telling us about the importance of praying at least once a day and never forgetting to thank Him for all His gifts.

"Before beginning your studies, always ask the Lord for help," declared French Father, looking up with reverence for God.

Thereupon, Gopal also looked up mockingly.

"Gopal, why are you turning your head upwards?" scolded French Father.

"I only want to see the Lord in the ceiling," talked back Gopal.

The whole class roared with laughter. French Father's face crimsoned with annoyance.

After decades of neglecting to brush up on my smattering of French, I decided to start learning the language once again. Some years ago, I wanted to enrol for a French course for foreigners in the nearby town of Draguignan, which is in the department of Var in the south of France.

"You're too old!" complained the French teacher. "You won't blend in with the other students who're all much younger."

A few weeks later, as I happened to be shopping in Draguignan, I just dropped into the language school and stood outside the French teacher's language classroom. While her class was in session, unnoticed by her, I quietly opened the door a tiny bit. What did I see? This middle-aged French lady was teaching French to a small group of elderly, white-skinned Europeans, some of them probably as old as me! I didn't dare to interrupt her while she was teaching and publicly accuse her of racism. In some countries, there is a lunatic fringe that can't stand living with coloured people, let alone teaching them. This was one of those rare instances in France when I felt that I had been discriminated against on the basis of colour, although in all fairness, it is quite possible that this French teacher had turned down my wish to be her pupil for other reasons. Perhaps she didn't like how I looked or the way I dressed. This bad experience put me off trying to learn French by means of attending classes.

I soon realised the importance of self-reliance. I knew that I should teach myself French with the help of books and magazines, and the guidance of Claudia, which was available at all times. By coincidence, I made the acquaintance of an English gentleman by the name of Alan Bancroft, who was self-taught in French. He mastered the new language and produced an excellent book called *Poems of St Thérèse of Lisieux*, translated by him. His ability to understand French well and even capture the subtle nuances in the French poetry of St Thérèse were a source of inspiration for me.

Trying to become proficient in French can be hard work. Yet, it has to be done.

Lots of times, my inadequate knowledge of French has landed me in trouble. During my early days in France, my vocabulary was so inadequate that I used to confuse '*notre*'—meaning ours—with '*votre*'—meaning yours. One day, when I ran into an acquaintance, I inquired after her son. I should have said, "Comment va votre fils?" Instead, I mistakenly said, "Comment va notre fils?"—"How is our son?" At first she looked embarrassed. Later, the poor lady gave me a grin.

Understanding written French is difficult enough, but who can make sense of the official version found in letters and notices from functionaries, in legal documents, and sometimes even in medical reports? At such times, from the depths of despair, I have regretted my decision to leave Australia and settle down in France following my retirement. If I return to Australia, I will no longer have to face the language-based problems that I have to suffer in France. But is it possible for an old man to uproot himself and move to down under in an instant? Travelling to that far-flung country would be a big upheaval bordering on trauma. Australia, I suppose, would be a relatively better and safer place to live only if there were a nuclear accident or war in Europe.

From time to time, both so-called friends and strangers have not hesitated to rebuke me for the mistakes I have made when trying to speak in French. They have never struck me with weapons of course, at least not yet, but they have attacked me with hurtful words. Psychologically speaking, injurious insults can often be as painful as physical blows. Those with sadistic traits, who detest me, for whatever reasons, use my errors in French as a pretext to express their simmering animosity towards me.

"Your articulation of French is awful!" remarked a post woman who was chatting with me for the first time. She was out on her rounds in an obscure village called Ferrières, which is in the Ariège département. I felt that her comment was uncalled for on that occasion.

"I'm a foreigner," I said, giving an explanation of why I mispronounced French words.

"But I know that you live here permanently," she continued.

"Do you also live here?" I asked.

"Yes," she replied. "When outsiders come here and buy houses, they must learn our language properly."

"Do you speak any other language?" I inquired.

"No," she snapped. "Why should I speak any other language when ours is the best?"

"Have you ever travelled abroad?" I asked.

"Never!" she said in a loud voice. "Why go abroad when France is the best country on the planet?"

"Vive la France!" I exclaimed.

She stared me in the face with suspicion.

Claudia and I travelled by train to Marseille to be present at the Cambodian Buddhist temple's *Vesak* ceremony on the full moon day of May. On this special day, every year, Buddhists celebrate three special events in the Buddha's life—his birth, Illumination, and demise at the age of eighty. While we were carrying on a conversation with a Cambodian Buddhist who spoke French fluently, the man unexpectedly started criticising me for failing to speak the language with the same free-flowing ease with which he expressed himself.

"You come from a country where the older generation still speak French," I remarked, defending myself from his fault-finding comments.

"It isn't that," he corrected me. "I've a flair for languages."

"I don't have your intelligence," I said.

This small and thin Cambodian gave us a haughty look and went away. Later that day, he apologised for his rudeness.

Every insult shatters the ego and temporarily reduces one to a state of nothingness. That is what happened to me when we were invited to lunch in the home of an elderly widow of means. She showed us all her precious objets d'art and ancient furniture. I particularly admired a period writing table of hers that had been a family heirloom for several generations.

"What's the French word for this?" I asked, pointing to it.

"Le bureau," she answered with a frown.

"I already know that word," I remarked. "But for some unknown reason, it had escaped me."

"Your mind isn't developed," she said suddenly, staring at me.

I was quite taken aback by her comment that obviously emanated from her highly developed mind.

Once, we were browsing through the large collection of interesting magazines and colourful Sunday papers at the news agent's in our little town. A few people gather there to exchange local gossip or meet friends. I was whispering something to Claudia in the tiny shop.

"Why do you always speak to your wife in English?" asked Henri, the shopkeeper, who seemed slightly annoyed with me.

"I speak in English because it's the greatest language," I retorted, making a provocative comment, and at the same time wondering about Henri's behaviour and his evidently antagonistic attitude towards English.

"I wish Henri would learn to mind his own business," I told Claudia while we were walking uphill towards our home. "Perhaps the man secretly enjoys listening to the conversations of his customers. Deprivation of some harmless fun from eavesdropping has upset the fellow."

With hindsight, I should have realised that Henri was not wrong after all. I would have made significant progress in French had the language we used at home been the official language of the land. Yet, at home we prefer to use English, which is the language that comes most naturally and easily to us. In this regard, we are like the Arabs who live and work in France: they prefer to use Arabic instead of French in their homes.

Despite the fact that we are not Christians, we read a

serious weekly called *Pèlerin* which has a strong Catholic bias. It discusses social, environmental, spiritual, and political issues in depth. There are difficult grammatical constructions in this weekly that I hope to understand with the passage of time; at present, I look new words up in the Robert Collins dictionary. I progress only at a snail's pace!

Right now, although I see the importance of knowing French well, alas, I lack the motivation to make an effort to achieve that end. The reason for this shortcoming is clear. I am not part of the labour force of France. I do not have to earn my livelihood in France, being a retiree who regularly receives a pension that comes from overseas. If I were a French functionary who had to clock in for office work in Paris every weekday and clock off in the evening, wouldn't I be straining every nerve to get a good command of French? Thank goodness, I'm not in a situation where I have to work for my bread and butter!

Imagine a worst-case scenario where the entire country is in a state of shock, following a violent coup d'état and a military takeover in Paris wherein democracy is discarded once and for all. The despot, the real ruler of France who lives in the Palais de l'Elysée, decrees that only French and no other language should henceforth be spoken in France, both in private and public places. Furthermore, he commands that anyone living in France, French-born or foreign-born, who fails to obey this decree will be guillotined. Even a life-threatening situation of this kind will not be an incentive for me to follow the decree. If such a coup comes to pass,

I will simply flee France. For that matter, if a fabulously wealthy person offers me twenty million Euros, provided I learn French in all its perfection, even the possibility of acquiring all that money is not going to change my half-hearted efforts to study this language. Besides, what can I do with all that money? I have enough to meet my modest daily expenses.

"With a good working knowledge of French, you'll be able to read and enjoy the works of great French writers," advised the owner of a French bookshop.

He was not wrong, but this advice came from an interested party.

"Today, it's possible to read fine English translations of nearly everything that's valuable in French literature," I observed. "Having said that, however, I'm not unaware that poetry doesn't translate well. Sometimes wit and humour are lost in translation. Nuances of meaning are also so difficult to translate. Therefore, it seems to me that to enter into the souls of French authors—their character, thoughts, feelings, and their invisible inner spirit—one has to read their works in the *original*."

"Absolutely," said the bookseller with a smile. "I couldn't agree more."

One of the best ways of promoting French throughout the world is to simplify the language, thereby making it considerably easier and quicker to learn. Archaic words and phrases can be replaced by less complicated ones that are easier to remember. For example, why not use the English word "please" for "s'il vous plait"? "Yours sincerely" is shorter and clearer than "veuillez agréer, Madame/Monsieur, l'expression de mes sentiments les meilleurs" or "je vous prie d'agréer, Madame/Monsieur, mes très respectueux hommages". Interestingly, some French-speaking nations like Belgium and Switzerland prefer "nonante" to the antiquated "quatre-vingt-dix".

Times change and one has to change with the times. If a language fails to bend, it will break. If it does not adapt itself to changing times, it soon gets discarded into the dustbin of history by the majority who use it. One is glad that widely used English words such as "breakfast", "stop", "weekend", "girlfriend" and "boyfriend" are already an integral part of French in the sense that they can be found more often in colloquial, everyday French. Fortunately, French is flexible despite the protests of purists who resent the presence of alien elements in modern French. It shows that French is a living and growing tongue that absorbs words and expressions from elsewhere. Is there any language in the world that is one-hundred per cent pure? Isn't every language an amalgam of different languages? So why do some people grumble about the fact that non-native words and phrases are slowly creeping into French?

The use and popularity of French in the world is unfortunately in decline, much to the chagrin of those who adore this language. Even in neighbouring Italy, for example, French is no longer the country's second language. English has replaced French. I have the impression that this is the case not only throughout the European Union, but also in nations that are not part of it, especially in distant powerful countries like Russia and China, where English has become their second language. All over the globe, fortunately or unfortunately, English is now the lingua franca. It is not French but English that has emerged as the principal language of commerce, science, and technology. It is a historical tendency that cannot be drastically curtailed or changed.

A thousand years hence, when we are no longer here, it is more than a mere theoretical possibility that English would have replaced French as France's official language. I realise that such a forecast would surely sound rather ridiculous to most French citizens. If I were still alive ten centuries from today, a very unlikely event, I would probably be quite saddened to see the demise of French with its immense literature of inestimable value. Perhaps it would be better not to speculate about this matter. Instead, let us pay attention to present-day problems.

It is a pity that in French schools not enough time is devoted to the teaching of English. When the next generation of French men and women start applying for jobs in different lands, much more than ever before because of the dearth of employment in the land of their birth, how will they fare? Unless they have an excellent command of English, they will not be able to compete with foreigners for the best jobs. In other words, they will be at a great disadvantage in the future.

Often enough, I am disappointed that many French people, who are supposedly educated, have only a rudimentary knowledge of English. They know next to nothing about English authors and their works. I am even more shocked that sometimes, they appear to have no regrets whatsoever about this huge gap in their knowledge. The French, let's take pity on them, don't know what they're missing!

I have met many elderly French citizens who have a very low opinion of the English. When will they transcend their ancient animosity towards their northern neighbour? This is a question that should prick the conscience of the French: how long will they be feuding with the British? Isn't it high time the French forget their past quarrels and make up with the British? The British, too, it goes without saying, must let go of their lingering feelings of dislike for the French. A lasting reconciliation between these two great nations is long overdue. Why not bring about a change of heart and set an example for the rest of humanity?

It has long been believed that the feeling of nationalism, which implies absolute loyalty to one's country of birth, is one of the greatest virtues. But is it really so? We have to call into question this time-honoured and widespread belief because history teaches us how nationalism, also called patriotism, has fuelled endless conflicts between otherwise friendly human beings, how it has led to numerous bloody wars and the resultant deaths, widespread destruction and environmental damage. Why have we forgotten that nationalism grew out of the seed of selfishness?

We frown upon selfishness with all its crudeness and primitive nature, especially when this ugly trait manifests itself. Self-centredness is often seen in growing children and grown-up adults. If we must disapprove of selfishness, we should, by the same token, also object to nationalism. Why do we fail to see that the so-called virtue of nationalism is nothing but our selfishness writ large?

In the past, nationalism has been glorified all over the world, particularly in history books, ignoring the truth that nationalism is only an expression of our individual selfishness en masse. Whether a crime is committed by an individual alone or together with others, isn't it still a crime? Motivated by greed and patriotic fervour, soldiers have killed, colonised, and exploited the helpless in various parts of the world. Are such deeds fundamentally different from those of a murderer who single-handedly kills a tourist and takes his purse?

We should realise the essential oneness of all human beings. Superficially, people of various lands are different in the sense that they don't look alike. Yet psychologically, we are exactly the same—we all suffer, we are all greedy, we are all proud, we all have hate, we all get frightened, and we are all aggressive. We are outwardly different but inwardly similar.

Once we outgrow our narrow nationalism, based on the myth that each and every nation has a distinct and distinguishable identity, and are therefore no longer asserting only the interests of any one single nation, we will inevitably have a *new* outlook on life, wherein we will start serving the common interests of humanity as a whole. Then our all-embracing love, if we are that sublime, would extend far beyond ourselves, our families, our countries, and even our planet. Then, having transcended the secular, we would be on the very threshold of the sacred.

9

CHARM OF
CHASTITY

The reactions of readers to this chapter heading can be easily foreseen.

"If the joy of sex is going to be removed, is life worth living?" many might ask with a deep sigh. "This crazy writer should surely know that without sex there wouldn't have been life in the first place. But because of sex, even this fool came into existence!" Such objections are only to be expected, given that throughout the ages we have been conditioned by our culture to believe that sexual activities are all part and parcel of everyday life. Hardly, if ever, do we call into question this perceived 'need' to engage in sex. Therefore, organised religions have sanctified sex by recognising the institution of marriage and societies have legalised it. In this way, we accept and respect sexual indulgence. Nowadays, as we all know, many practise sex out of wedlock. We regard it as legal, but not moral.

The sexual union of man and woman has long been seen as the norm; homosexuality and lesbianism have been thought of as departures from that set standard. Similarly, we can view masturbation as a deviation from the usual way of having sex. The writings of Marquis de Sade are replete with references to, and descriptions of, sexual perversions. Those who indulge in these so-called deviations would question the right of sexual intercourse between man and woman to be regarded as the norm. If we see one form of sexual indulgence as the norm, logically speaking, every other form of sexual indulgence would be a deviation or perversion. From the standpoint of Pope Leo X, Martin Luther was a heretic; but from Luther's standpoint, the real heretic was none other than the Pope himself. So can anyone be absolutely sure as to what right sexual conduct is and what is wrong or sinful sexual conduct?

One cannot understand why we frown upon some forms of sexual expression, while we consider sexual intercourse between men and women as being all right. Why do we have double standards? Aren't all forms of sexual actions essentially *the same*? For this reason, the chaste abstain from each and every kind of sexual deed.

There is a cynical saying, rightly or wrongly ascribed to George Bernard Shaw: "chastity is the lack of opportunity". Is that necessarily the case?

Let us consider the situation of monks and nuns who are bursting with lust—the poor devils can't help it—and are consequently struggling to hold it back because they are bound by vows of chastity. Would such desperate religious souls not want to taste forbidden fruit, doing so clandestinely of course, if the opportunity ever presents itself? What is eaten with relish, and on the sly, is not just tasty but a thousand times tastier than the nectar of the gods. These holy brothers and holy sisters can always rationalise their naughty behaviour by saying, "That's the way the Creator created me" or "the Lord implanted this lovely urge" and leave it at that.

At the other end of the spectrum are the very few whose chastity is whiter than the whiteness of a falling snowflake. Their purity is truly indescribable. For instance, persons of clean character never need to rack their brains, trying to decide whether to resist temptation or to give in to it. Every sexual opportunity will be a matter of complete indifference to them. They would even be bored with people who are preoccupied with sex, while at the same time pitying their plight; they would also regard sexual or scatological humour as the pathological product of perverted psyches.

In 1935, Mahatma Gandhi remarked insightfully that since youth is a priceless possession, it should not be squandered away for the sake of a "momentary excitement, miscalled pleasure". Even adults can take heed of his advice because in the modern world, more and more people are taking pride in their sexual promiscuity, and even boasting about their sexual conquests, thus dissipating their time and energies instead of devoting them to socially useful or spiritually uplifting pursuits.

Our earth, alas, is littered with libertines. Yet once in a blue moon, one can still meet married couples who, because they lead chaste lives, are glad that they are not chained all day to the tasks and responsibilities entailed in raising children. If a woman has an uncontrollable urge to bring up a child, she can give expression to her maternal instinct by adopting a parentless child or an abandoned little one, rather than give birth to a baby in this overpopulated planet of ours. A childless female is likely to have more time at her disposal, and perhaps more stamina as well, than one with youngsters in her charge. The additional leisure time can be set aside for charitable and creative work, not to mention what are called the things of the mind and spirit.

What is today's most urgent need? The prime requirement is a much smaller population with a superior intellectual and moral standard instead of a burgeoning community of an inferior kind. Let us place a premium on quality in lieu of quantity.

From time to time, both known and unknown people seek my advice. Eager to find solutions to their various problems and difficulties, they contact me in the hope of getting a sympathetic ear. I try my best to help them, in spite of the fact that my suggestions are sometimes not to their liking. If it is a medical problem, I usually refer them to trained specialists, although I must confess that sometimes I do propose rough and ready home remedies for simple ailments. That is a dangerous thing to do. Who am I to decide whether an illness is a simple or a complicated one? Amateurs can, and often do, misread symptoms.

One day, I received a letter from Rudolph (not his real

name). The young man was deeply troubled by a private and perhaps embarrassing difficulty. The sense of urgency in his letter called for a prompt and detailed reply. The correspondence speaks for itself:

Dear Susunaga

I couldn't email you for some time because I couldn't contact you, so how are you? I read all the books you sent me. All are good stories so now I like to read one of your other books about meditation because I like to do meditation but I have no idea of how to begin, so I think you would help me with your experience.

I think I mentioned you that I'm a gay and I want to get rid of it now, so I think meditation will help me for getting rid of that bad habit.

I'm asking you to send me one of your books on meditation.

With best wishes
Rudolph Engelberger

Dear Rudolph

In a recent letter, you referred to a big worry: "I think meditation will help me for getting rid of that bad habit." This comment relates to your being a gay.

Yes, meditation will definitely be a great help. Please study the chapters on meditation in the three books of mine which I posted you last week (Nirvana the Highest

Happiness, The First and Best Buddhist Teachings *and* Serenity Here and Now). *These are presents for the New Year.*

It is important not to have a condemnatory attitude when examining a habit. If you have a guilty mind, then simply be aware of that sense of guilt. On the other hand, it is not good to think that there is nothing wrong with being a gay. I mean, neither condemn nor justify it. One has to look at each and every sexual inclination impartially. In your case, you need to be neither against homosexuality nor for it. Neither be ashamed of your homosexuality nor be proud of it (many gays try to justify their condition by thinking "some distinguished men of letters like Oscar Wilde and Somerset Maugham were also gays"). Just see your difficulty as a fact, without telling yourself "how horrible!" or "how wonderful!" Only then will it become possible to understand this problem correctly. Unfortunately, I have just used the wrong word by calling it a problem. Please do not regard it as a problem! It is only a trait, like any other trait, such as a person's liking for cigarettes, beer or arrack.

Many years ago, I had a friend, Edith Ludowyk, who was one of the leading psychoanalysts in the world; in fact, this lady had been a student and later a friend of the great Sigmund Freud. She used to say, "Why does lesbianism and homosexuality shock or surprise people? Don't they realise that every human being is the biological product of a man and a woman? You must, therefore, expect to find in each individual both feminine and masculine tendencies."

Once, I was discussing this subject with a Buddhist monk. He observed that a good many homosexuals had been women in their previous lives. It is extremely difficult, even impossible, to recall our past lives; yet, I have met a few persons with the remarkable ability to remember the details of some of their former incarnations.

Is it possible to be exactly sure about the psychological origins of any of our numerous inclinations? We can only speculate about why we have certain likes or dislikes. But, if through meditation, one manages to trace the sources of our likes and dislikes, it is probable that at least a few of our hidden passions, once their beginnings are thus uncovered, might drop off once and for all. This is what happened to Kelaart in my novel Sunil the Struggling Student.

I used to know a gay person, a school teacher, who is no longer alive. When he was a child, his mother left him when she found a new lover, a handsome and wealthy young man. In other words, the mother abandoned both her son and her husband, and went to live with her new lover. Her behaviour resulted in the boy losing interest not only in his mother, but in all women. He distrusted all women; in fact, he started hating all girls and women. The boy's mind suddenly became anti-female, and his resentment of females remained throughout his life. This pathological prejudice never went away. It turned him into a gay. All his life, he tried to extricate himself from his fondness for males, but the more he struggled, the stronger became his craving for sexual encounters with boys and men.

Fighting an inner urge naturally and inevitably results in its reinforcement. For example, what happens if a person tries to repress his anger? Repression only adds fuel to the anger. Admittedly, the expression of anger does give some temporary relief, but the briefly subdued anger continues to remain in a magnified form. Any attempt to trample down your ill temper causes its re-emergence in a greatly strengthened manifestation. One cannot strangle rage, the sexual urge or any emotion for that matter. What then, is one to do? My short and simple answer is DO NOTHING BUT JUST WATCH IT. The mere act of watching the mind passively, without interfering with it in any way, is the cardinal characteristic of meditation.

I knew another man, also a school teacher, who became a gay for a similar reason. After the deaths of his parents when he was a little child, Robert was raised by several doting aunts. All these ladies were strict disciplinarians. They were domineering women, although well-meaning ones; they never failed to shower the lad with affection. What was the consequence of this excessive interest in their nephew? Overpowered by their constant attention, the boy reacted by yearning for independence. He grew up with a fear of members of the opposite sex. When his sexual feelings started arising during his adolescence, this youth discovered that he was greatly attracted to boys instead of girls. All his life, Robert remained a gay through and through.

I also remember a conversation I once had with a handsome young man in his thirties, an accountant who lived alone in Colombo.

"Whenever I see the face or the breasts of a woman, I think of my late mother—the sweetest woman God ever created for she was the personification of love and goodness," he said, wiping a tear and gazing into the roaring waves of the Indian Ocean. *"I simply can't bring myself to take a woman to bed, for wouldn't that be like taking my own beloved mother to bed? What a disgusting idea! When it comes to sex, any day I'd prefer a man, preferably a sweet young boy."*

Throughout my student days, it used to be my practice to discuss every subject under the sun with other students and strangers; we did so without any inhibitions whatsoever. No topic was taboo at that time and we explored everything with enthusiasm.

"What deters me from having a sexual relationship with a girl is the fear that she might become pregnant," confessed a young university student in London. *"I definitely don't want to father a child with all the headaches and expenses that go with such a responsibility. But my mind is not weighed down by such worries whenever I have sex with a fellow male student, which I do from time to time."*

"Is that the only reason for avoiding physical relationships with females?" I asked.

"No, there's always the risk of getting syphilis or some such deadly venereal disease from a girl," he replied.

"What makes you think that such dangers don't exist when you sleep with men?" I argued.

"Yes, you've a point," he remarked pensively. "But when I meet a charming guy such thoughts don't occur to me!"

Dear Rudolph, please don't think that I'm trying to dissuade you from your carnal interest in males and persuade you to start chasing females for a change. That, clearly, is not my intention. I only wish to open your eyes so that you can start viewing sexual indulgence in a new light. If I succeed in doing that, your whole attitude to all forms of sexual activity might undergo a fundamental transformation.

The ingenuity of people is so great that over the ages, men and women have discovered a thousand different ways to express their innate sexuality. Is it an improvement for a gay to give up being a homosexual and become a heterosexual or vice versa? Is it a sign of progress if an alcoholic stops taking whisky and starts drinking vodka instead? However, in the above-mentioned instance, we can say that an extraordinary change surely takes place when an alcoholic desists from taking any kind of alcohol whatsoever; similarly, when a homosexual lets go of not only his homosexuality, but all forms of sexuality, it can be rightly said that he has undergone a total metamorphosis in his life.

What is most valuable in life? Freedom from every manifestation of sexuality is the hallmark of a truly civilised person. Those who are enslaved by any kind of sexuality—be it homosexuality, heterosexuality or any kind of carnal gratification—have yet to transcend their primitive, animalistic nature.

We must ask ourselves a basic question: What is Mother

Nature's purpose in implanting in us the sexual instinct? None can disagree that the sole purpose of sex is reproduction. In other words, the reason for this instinct is nothing but procreation, not recreation. So great is our degeneration that we have abused this instinct and turned it into a source of pleasure, and a means of escaping from the struggles and sorrows of life.

Someday you might meet a female who is affectionate, intelligent, and excellent in other respects. There is no harm in marrying someone like that, provided you have with that woman a close relationship. It is possible to be extremely happy while leading a sexually abstemious life.

In my youth, I had the good fortune to know a great sage and yogi by the name of Swami Sivananda of Rishikesh in the Himalayas. This saintly and dynamic person was a distinguished doctor, who, while writing hundreds of books, had the time to attend to the needs of his many patients, doing so free of charge. I feel impelled to mention his name because Sivananda led a chaste life. As a result of his clean lifestyle, the man became strong and energetic. He enjoyed good health, although he never managed to overcome his diabetes. He had considerable compassion for all human beings and animals. With no sexual problems to distract or disturb his mind, Sivananda was able to use his tons of talents and vivacity for the benefit of mankind.

Nowadays, even in the Indian world, generally speaking, it has become the fashion to scoff at the ancient ideal of Brahmacharya: the requirement to be celibate in thought, word, and deed. Sivananda wrote a famous book on this subject that is worth reading. Sexual energy can be sublimated and used for noble ends. You can express your creativity with redoubled vigour once this energy is conserved and not wasted. You may, for instance, use it for delving deeply into subjects that interest you in any field, especially in those of literature, art, and music; perhaps you can become a social worker and thereby help the less privileged sections of society. You can become a voracious reader, a globetrotter or dedicate your life to psychological purification via meditation. Even if you never achieve anything of social significance, it does not matter so long as you end up becoming thoroughly pure—free from everything that is negative within yourself such as anger, hate, resentment, avarice, greed, vanity, and pride. It will be enough of an achievement if an individual can at least blossom into a decent human being whose life is in accord with the highest moral standards.

Your happiness should not be dependent on the persons who are close to you in life, be it your spouse or partner. That is to say, you should be yourself the sole source of happiness, for it is possible that you might never meet someone who is a suitable companion for your particular temperament. So be prepared for the likelihood of having to remain single all your life. There is a saying ascribed to the Buddha: in the journey of life it is better to walk alone than to have a fool as a companion.

If you cease being gay, what is likely to happen? I think you would suddenly enjoy great peace of mind, being no longer troubled by the conflicts, quarrels, and misunderstandings that had invariably spoilt your relationships with sexual partners in the past. Whereas your feelings for men were once probably based on pure lust, you will find that you have changed greatly: pure love has replaced pure lust.

When selfless and celestial love becomes the guiding force in your life, for the first time you will be able to have deep affection for men and women in quite a different way. You will, for one thing, never again regard other human beings as mere sexual objects—just a source of satisfaction for your animalistic urges. Ceasing sexual involvements of every kind in the years to come will indeed be a sea change.

An orgasm is nothing more than a short-lived nervous titillation. It is all over in a split second, leaving you exhausted and shattered in both body and mind. Unless Mother Nature had implanted in man and beast this instinct to behave insanely for just a passing moment, the process of ceaseless creation would have been brought to a halt. When Mother Nature put in us this drive, she was surely tricking us into becoming involved in sexual activity. Therefore, we have the choice of either becoming enslaved by Mother Nature or rather defying her and thus becoming masters of our own destiny.

Some decades ago, the word 'gay' referred to the pleasant state of being cheerful, excited or happy; today, however, we use this unfortunate word when we are talking about homosexuals or their activities—gay bars, gay parades, gay rights and so forth.

I have shown that it is possible to be happy and celibate at the same time, transcending both heterosexual and homosexual tendencies.

There is a sex-free spiritual realm of sheer joy that only some secure.

Wishing you good luck,
Susunaga

10

KRISHNAMURTI'S
COMMENTS
ON SEX

In his remarkable book titled *The First and Last Freedom*, J. Krishnamurti (1895-1986), a sage of great insight, made some observations on sex which are thought-provoking. Let us consider just a few of his comments.

Why are we obsessed with sex? Why has sex become such a central issue in our lives? What is the essence of the problem of sex? It is hardly the sexual act, is it? Surely is it not the act per se, but *thinking* about sex that causes so many difficulties and a hundred headaches? Given our thought-centred or cerebral temperament, this thought-created situation is inevitable. The influence of mass media, cinema, literature, and the way we dress are also factors that stimulate the mind and strengthen our preoccupation with sex.

Everything we do in life, explains Krishnamurti, is designed to give emphasis to the 'me'. We are egotistical creatures in the sense that we are anything but loving and altruistic. It is nothing but our vain and self-seeking or self-serving nature that makes us unhappy.

For this reason, we ceaselessly try to break through the barriers of the self, this sense of 'me', hoping, thereby, to find some degree of happiness, which is the feeling of relief experienced whenever one manages to get beyond the imprisoning confines of the self. Now, why has sex become so pathologically important for us? Sex affords us a means of sheer self-forgetfulness, even though the orgasmic experience is so sadly short-lived. How people treasure those few seconds when they temporarily succeed in escaping fully from themselves! When getting away from the feeling of 'I am', 'me' or the self, the theistically inclined like to think that they are standing on the doorstep of the Divine; others claim to have had fleeting glimpses of the Infinite. Those who meditate are well aware that we rationalise our sexual behaviour, not to mention our weakness for the grandiose.

Without understanding the ways of the mind we cannot fully get to grips with the problem of sex. Often, we inadvertently fuel the sense of 'me' through our various self-expansionary thoughts, words, and deeds on the one hand, and try to lose ourselves momentarily by means of sex on the other. How few are aware of this paradoxical situation! This matter, according to Krishnamurti, cannot be solved by the mind because the mind itself is the problem, as we shall see presently.

Problems cease only when the self is transcended. That state in which the 'me' is absolutely absent cannot be brought about by an act of will; it cannot be artificially created.

Chastity is not a virtue that can be carefully cultivated as many religious persons naively imagine. The repression of sexual desire is not chastity. Nor is sexual expression the solution. Repression not only intensifies lust, but also fortifies the will which is the handmaiden of the ego. Those who repress become self-controlled, stern, strict, and hard. They inevitably develop a strong sense of power. One can notice some of these traits in highly disciplined ascetics. Therefore, when sexual persons practise chastity, their subsequent behaviour is not without carnal qualities; they are still governed and driven by sensual appetites, whereas genuine chastity blossoms spontaneously and effortlessly, but that happens only when there is selfless love.

Unalloyed affection, mind you, is never the product of the mind. This means that true chastity is hardly the outcome of a pious vow. It cannot be foisted on a postulant by the head of a convent, monastery or temple. There is much truth in the old proverb that the cowl does not make the monk. Nor do religious resolutions make monks and nuns chaste unless they take the trouble to meditate and transcend all their self-centred traits.

The very same observations can be made about pride, vanity or arrogance. When a proud person 'practises' humility, what really happens? Being so saturated with thoughts and feelings of self-importance, pride is incapable of becoming humility. Those who cultivate such a so-called humility only continue, in a modified manner, to express their latent pride, which is now a mere projection of pride under the guise of humbleness. One can, in fact, say this of *all* virtues. Virtues cannot be likened to plants that grow taller and bigger over a period of time; on the contrary, the whole range of virtues suddenly appears once one lets go of the ego. Unfortunately, this miracle of a change rarely happens. But, if and when it does, ordinary human beings become extraordinary. Even savages metamorphose into saints.

In a gripping book by Rom Landau on modern mystics, masters, and teachers, which is titled *God is My Adventure*, Krishnamurti openly declared that he personally got as much joy from affectionately touching the hand of a person he was fond of as another might obtain from having sex.

Let us examine the profound implications of Krishnamurti's statement. First, when the whole of their being is suffused with pure and unselfish love or limitless and ceaseless compassion, highly evolved individuals are never troubled by the sexual instinct. Second, since they are immersed in ethereal ecstasies, they are not drawn to the gross demands and gratifications of the genitals.

Whenever Krishnamurti talked about himself, one could get a good glimpse of the sage's inner state. His was a rare spiritual dimension in which universal love had replaced personal love. He had the same affection for all, no matter whether the person who called on him was a perfect stranger or an old friend. Love for him was a constant state within himself and he could not help loving everyone he met. There weren't any that he particularly disliked. He would feel a certain mystical unity not only with human beings, but also with the trees, sky, and mountains, including every living creature and everything in the entire world that surrounded him.

Among the profound perceptions of Krishnamurti, his various virtues, and the interesting events in his life, all of which I have discussed at length in my book *J. Krishnamurti as I Knew Him*, the following is a typical example of his sheer selflessness.

Out of the goodness of his heart, Krishnamurti spontaneously gave a beggar his clothes as a present. Without any regret whatsoever, he would readily part with any or all of his personal effects. He had no sense of possession or ownership. He never felt that anything really belonged to him. That exalted state sprang from the fact that his sense of 'me', 'mine' or 'I', with all its small-minded heartlessness, had ceased to exist.

Rare indeed are mystics who chance upon the state of super consciousness and experience the eternal peace and happiness of the celestial. Sexual pleasures mean nothing to them now. Those transient thrills put them off once and for all. For what those other-worldly few have found is incomparably *more* satisfying and superior to what the vulgar world would offer.

Let us examine a view about sex that is widely held. There are many who maintain that sexual relationships between men and women are all right, provided sex is seen as an expression of love. If it is love that cements a relationship, it is well and good. That love alone is enough to sustain the relationship during all the vicissitudes of life. Since the connection between the parties is already well established, if that is, in fact, the case, why the need to shore up the affection-based bond by means of sex? Those who declare that sex is an expression of love are, more often than not, trying to justify their insatiable craving for sex. They know how to use this clever excuse to disguise their feelings for a bit of rumpy-pumpy.

We are not questioning the importance of love in our lives. Love is a *sine qua non* for peace, harmony, and goodwill in all societies. We are in such a mess because of the almost total absence of pure love in both the individual and the world at large.

What is the nature of pure love? It is surely to love a man or woman for that person's own sake, loving and caring to *give* him or her all advantages, be they material or spiritual, but concerned *never to use* that human being, be it for sex or any other purpose.

Whenever a human relationship is soiled because there is a sexual dimension to it, there will be conflicts, complications, and misunderstandings. Not being weighed down by time-wasting and energy-depleting disputes with lovers or sexual partners, the chaste find peace of mind, and consequently, become clear-sighted. Such intelligence is a great asset to those wishing to meditate and lead a spiritual life.

In conclusion, it is necessary to refer to the fact that the writer of this essay is a happily married man who has been leading a sexually abstemious life for several decades, and is all the more happier, healthier, stronger, and wiser for just this one reason.

11

WHAT IS BEST AND FINE FOR LEISURE TIME?

What is best and fine for one person might not be so for another. Needless to say, each individual has to decide for himself or herself the leisure activities that are most suitable to them, taking into consideration such factors as one's age, gender, state of health, occupation, and the time available for doing things that are enjoyable and relaxed. Having made it clear that what you wish to do in your spare time is a purely private and personal matter, even a question of particular taste, I shall proceed to write briefly about how my leisure time is spent, not that it is of enormous importance, but the reader could find in this short piece of writing some useful hints on augmenting the joy of living.

There is a relaxed atmosphere at dawn. Seeing how the darkness disappears as the light of the sun begins to appear in the firmament makes one feel cheerful. This glorious sight gives one a lot of confidence.

"Oh, that happens every day!" the sceptic might say, trying to belittle the splendour of sunrises and sunsets. Many do not care to observe the skies that are extraordinarily beautiful at sunrise and sunset.

Once again, this morning, I noticed how suddenly the skies turned crimson. There were other hues around the swiftly emerging ball of fire, but deep red was the predominant colour. Only for a very short time, alas, were the eastern skies awash with many colours. The exquisite hues faded away quickly and ordinary daylight prevailed.

At this early hour, the air is particularly fresh. It is the best time to take a few deep and exhilarating breaths, provided the air is pure. It is usually clean and not yet polluted by drivers who start revving their motor vehicles before driving off to work. I love to practise *Pranayama* (yogic breathing exercises) during this short period. These simple exercises ensure good health and longevity.

How many visitors to art galleries across the world, while eagerly frequenting exhibitions to see invaluable paintings, also take the trouble to rise early and marvel over the beauty of a sunrise? They flock to museums to enjoy the sight of masterpieces made by the hand of man that adorn the walls, forgetting the mysterious beauty of sunrises and sunsets, which deserve to be regarded as Mother Nature's masterpieces. Some galleries charge exorbitant entrance fees, but all the creations of Mother Nature can be viewed and enjoyed free of charge by one and all.

I love walking along quiet country footpaths in which only pedestrians are allowed. But walking on the crowded pavements of towns and cities can be counterproductive—

there is the risk of inhaling dangerous exhaust fumes and of traffic noises disrupting what could otherwise be an undisturbed walk. Country roads are best because while strolling along them, one can listen to the singing of birds and the croaking of frogs. Man-made noises are not conducive to calm; they do not steady the nerves. The sounds of animals, on the other hand, are hardly an annoyance. I find the sound of a car screeching to a halt far more trying than the noise of a barking dog.

The green, soothing, and uplifting scenery that one can savour while roaming country roads is another reason why country walks are more pleasant than walking on urban streets where there is usually a dearth of awe-inspiring scenery or lovely landscapes. As I live in a rural area, I am used to being in silent neighbourhoods, but on the rare occasions when I visit big cities like Paris or Marseille, the experience of fighting my way through the throngs often leaves me fatigued.

One of the joys of walking is the possibility of leaving the mind to its own devices, so to speak, so that it can think whatever it wants. The mind needs the freedom to wander aimlessly. That is a form of relaxation. This kind of mental repose is easier in relatively calm country lanes. But in crowded places, how can the mind be in a tensionless state if the entire time one has to be wary of pickpockets and careless drivers?

What is going to be described below can take place either while walking in a quiet village or on the busy streets of a metropolis that is bustling with people.

Imagine a contemplative gentleman who loves to lead a solitary life. While he is out on a long walk, he runs into a garrulous lady, who invites the gentleman for a drink. The man accepts the offer. While having refreshments, the woman insists on having a long conversation with the gentleman.

"It's nice of you to invite me for a drink, but I like to be alone," says the man, sipping his wine. "Without speaking to anyone, I just like to observe what others are doing in a relaxed atmosphere. In this way, I get to know this place better. But thanks for the drink."

"Then I'll say goodbye," snaps the spurned lady in an angry voice. Then, she springs to her feet and walks off in a huff.

It is obvious that walking exercises the leg muscles. However, there is a consensus among doctors that walking tones up the *entire* body. It is good for the heart; it prevents insomnia, backache, haemorrhoids, and other medical problems. Regardless of the weather, be it sunny or stormy, a health-conscious individual never forgets his or her constitutional stroll. In an essay on leisure time, the question of good health is not an irrelevant one: the better your health the greater the enjoyment of your leisure time.

So strong is my passion for certain kinds of music that I could devote every minute of my leisure time to hearing good renderings of them. It is not with the intention of hastening my spiritual unfolding that I like to listen to sacred music from each and every religious source. But if I happen to hear organ music, especially the works of Handel, J. S. Bach, Beethoven, Haydn or Telemann, my spirits rise from their dormant condition and start moving towards exalted states of consciousness. For want of a better way of putting it, I would say that devotional music provides an opportunity for self-purification, with the accumulated defilements of every day effortlessly dropping off one by one as a result of the intense devotion that such music inspires.

In recent years, I have developed a taste for Carnatic music from the Indian sub-continent. I must confess that I have not studied the theoretical or technical aspects of Carnatic music. But the experience of listening sympathetically to it, keeping one's ears open to the repetitious use of certain sounds and words, culminates in experiencing blissful states that defy description.

In Indian Bhakti music, one's love is directed towards a personal deity or a holy person. There is also the music that springs from being in a loving state, but here, one's love is not focused on a personal deity, saint, pious individual or any sacred object for that matter. This kind of music is usually about the Absolute, which can be described as the sphere in which there are no restrictions. It is the Unconditioned or the Ultimate that is so free that it is not, in any way, connected to any person or thing. This music expresses love or devotion per se. It is usually instrumental.

Gardening can be a pleasant way of spending one's free time, provided a gardening session does not go on for more than about ninety minutes. Beyond this time, the work can make one extremely tired.

I do simple jobs like weeding, mowing the lawns, raking fallen leaves, and trimming the hedges; my wife plants seedlings, and grows fruits and vegetables without the use of chemical fertilisers and pesticides in the course of doing organic gardening. We produce the compost that is needed and supplement it with animal dung. Much of the water that is necessary for the plants comes from the rain water that we collect in several tanks; this water is cleaner than the chlorinated water from the taps. There are times when we have to work hard together, such as during the olive picking season in December. Most of the olive oil we use every year comes from our very own olive trees. We have the satisfaction of knowing that this oil is pure and of good quality. We also have to work under pressure during the short-lived cherry season when there is an abundance of these delicious fruits. Such is Mother Nature's munificence that she gives us far more fruits than what we actually need and we give away most of the cherries to people we know and also to strangers on the streets.

What a pity that the tasty tropical fruits I used to relish in my early years, such as pawpaw, mangoes, pineapples, and bananas do not grow in the south of France! In compensation, Mother Nature produces a few figs, some Mirabelle fruits (small yellow plums), persimmons, and hazelnuts.

The upkeep of the garden has to continue throughout

the year. I have heard a local gardener remark that gardens are like women: you have to give them your undivided attention all the time to get the best results. He was, without doubt, very knowledgeable about both gardening and the ways of women!

"When all is said and done," a critic might derisively ask, "was it worth all your effort, energy, and time? Couldn't you have bought all that you've so laboriously grown in any shop selling organic fruits and vegetables?"

"Yes, I could," I would answer. "But the deep feeling of contentment that comes from having done something creative during leisure time is of inestimable value."

We think that gardening of this sort cannot be carried out unless there is a loving relationship between the plants and us, which creates its own joy.

When I feel the need to relax, I like to read newspapers, magazines, novels, and books with short stories. Both fictional and non-fictional works interest me as long as they are not too heavy. Light reading is excellent to unwind when I am feeling tired or stressed. To keep myself fully informed about current affairs, I read a reliable newspaper. I go through it at a slow pace, skipping any item that does not interest me. I am attracted to articles that discuss subjects in depth. So, I have given up watching TV news where topics are examined on a superficial level. The worst is when the newsreader reads out the news reports at breakneck speed and when I am forced to listen to matters that bore me. I store away articles of perennial interest for future reading.

Whenever I read a newspaper, periodical or book, I like to keep an etymological dictionary open by my side. This I do regularly since I am keen on knowing the origins and different meanings of words. This is a favourite pastime of mine.

In conclusion, I would like to refer to the form of relaxation that I like most. On afternoons when the weather is not rainy, windy or stormy, we go to the seaside resort of Saint Raphael that borders the Mediterranean. After finding a quiet and pleasant spot on the beach, we stretch our tired legs on the summery sand and settle in for a short sleep. Once we have been through this ritual, we are alert and ready to watch the graceful movements of the huge white seagulls that hover above the surface of the waves and the seemingly endless sandy stretches. Sometimes we succeed in catching these birds' attention by offering them tiny pieces of hard dry bread. The elegant and angelic creatures make a quick dive for the food, take hold of the morsels of bread in their beaks, and fly away slowly. Feeding them is great fun.

While sitting on the sand, it is fascinating to see the deep blue cloudless skies and the immense sea right in front of us. We see a dark steamer on the horizon, the illusory line where the sky and the ocean seem to meet.

It is enthralling to gaze into space and realise that we are smaller than even an insignificant speck in the vast universe. While doing so, we suddenly become conscious of the limitlessness of space and time. That humbling awareness enables us to get a glimpse of infinity. The mind, too, reaches that realm of nothingness and loses itself. At that very moment, while transcending the mind, we make an entrance into the Celestial Sphere.

12

BOOKS AND
SOLITUDE ARE
THE BEST FRIENDS

On this sad occasion, I have come to pay my last respects to our dear-departed Gerda von Fellenberg.

Although I am the son-in-law of Gerda, we somehow managed to get along peacefully and harmoniously. Gerda and I have something else in common. Both of us happen to be authors.

In my opinion, Gerda was a remarkable writer. Although in her lifetime only four of her manuscripts were published, she has left behind for the world a great big mass of manuscripts. She authored autobiographical novels, a play for the stage, a radio play, essays, and poems. Gerda would write to newspapers on controversial subjects. All these interesting manuscripts are now preserved in the Burgerbibliothek in Bern, which is situated in Münstergasse, and can be read by the public.

Once I offered to get one of her manuscripts published in India. "Many thanks," she said, "but I can't accept your kind offer. You see, I write for future generations. My writings will be appreciated only after I have passed away."

Gerda was an extremely serious person. But even when her face had a grave expression, she was able to see the funny side of things; she was able to enjoy a good laugh.

Gerda developed her literary talents by following a course in creative writing at Schule des Schreibens in Munich. She became a prolific writer, devoting most of her time and energy to reading and writing. Books and solitude were her best friends. She was happiest when she was alone to pursue her literary work. She enjoyed her solitary walks in quiet places. She loved to commune with Mother Nature. Gerda was particularly fond of flowers and children, especially children who were disabled in body or mind. Until the end of her life, she never stopped caring for her handicapped daughter, Heidi.

Like every great writer of previous centuries, Gerda was a voracious reader. The range of her reading extended from Lao-tse and the Buddha in the East to Meister Eckhart and Karl Gustav Jung in the West. It is necessary to mention the names of some of her favourite writers—Pessoa, Josef Roth, Jean Améry, Goethe, of course, Marguerite Duras, Somerset Maugham, Virginia Woolf, and Guy de Maupassant. Some of her favourite philosophers were Schopenhauer and Martin Buber. Gerda herself was a philosopher in her own right, in the sense that she lived a life that was true and faithful to her deepest convictions.

Where is Gerda now? I wish I knew the answer to that question. Like all of you who are Christians, I would also wish that she is in heaven or in some celestial world. As a Buddhist, I sincerely hope that someday she succeeds in finding for herself the supreme peace and happiness of Nirvana.

A tribute by Susunaga Weeraperuma to Gerda von Fellenberg on the occasion of her funeral (11 December, 2012) at the Kirche St Josef, Köniz, near Bern, Switzerland.

13

WHY NOT BE RELAXED AND HAPPY?

Far too many French men and women are apparently unable to cope with the stress of being underemployed. Even the lucky ones with jobs are stressed. Both the moneyed and the penniless have feelings of anxiety. Many have neither spouses nor partners. Some are lone parents. Hélas! They look so worried and anxious, taking puffs from their cigarettes several times a day or drinking wine to relieve unpleasant thoughts and feelings for the time being. No amount of make-up can disguise their worn-out appearances caused by insufficient sleep. Why do they have to rush through their domestic chores or struggle daily with their workloads as though they were running fast to be in time for the train? Why are people so fidgety, so incapable of staying still or moving slowly? Signs of restlessness can be seen in most people. I have no facts or figures to back up these sweeping generalisations, but it doesn't matter. Readers can decide for themselves whether my conclusions are correct or not.

Do I give the impression that I don't rely heavily on statistics? Well, that is true, but to buttress an argument, I occasionally use statistics, availing myself of them only when it is absolutely necessary to do so. It is a great pity that the media gives so much importance to statistics. Why do I have this distrust of statistics? There is the fear that statistics-based thinking might weaken or even atrophy one's inherent powers of observation. Besides, one remembers the famous comment attributed to Disraeli: "There are three kinds of lies: there are lies, damned lies, and statistics." Therefore, the conclusions drawn by statisticians are not of prime importance.

What then is of foremost significance? Can't we ourselves directly find out what this so-called marvellous world of ours is really like by means of our sense organs—seeing, smelling, hearing, tasting, and feeling? Must we not make active our dormant non-cerebral faculties of knowing?

This discussion, alas, has drifted from stress to statistics. So let us go back to looking at the causes of the stresses and strains of everyday life.

When Marie-Beatrice jilted her long-time fiancé, Henri, just before their planned wedding in a posh Paris restaurant, poor Henri was understandably upset. His disturbed state resulted in stress. It was followed by sleepless nights and a mental breakdown.

When Lawrence, the long-experienced manager of a grocery store, was given the sack, he was absolutely furious. At the age of forty-five, he did not stand a chance of getting a good job. Great was his sense of frustration. Believing that he could relieve his stress by hitting the bottle, Lawrence started frequenting bars. He soon became the victim of liver cirrhosis. Similarly, the thousands of workers in factories and elsewhere who are suddenly made redundant through no fault of theirs, these helpless people also become prone to stress at first, and sometime later, to stress-related illnesses. Such calamities seem endemic in all capitalistic societies, and not merely in France, that cannot guarantee employees permanent and lifelong employment.

Quite early in life, weak and fragile Christine, a Parisian, was already aware of her unsuitability for manual or menial work. For this reason, she was keen on getting a higher education. But when her final attempt to pass the baccalaureate failed, it dashed her hopes even to get a first degree. Deeply distressed, she started smoking cigarettes. Addicted to nicotine, she soon became a chain-smoker. "Without fags, I'll be saturated with strain," Christine once confessed to a close friend who had tried her best to dissuade Christine from smoking. Before long, the young lady was diagnosed with advanced breast cancer.

A stressed lady can take some sips of whisky and run away from stress for a short time; similarly, a man under stress can have a mistress and experience short spells of relief from time to time. Neither of them is taking a deep, long look at stress, rather, they are only evading it.

People who are stressed try to escape from it in various ways. Many like to become involved in what to them are interesting activities. They become busybodies because of their restless nature. The result of such hyperactivity is nervous exhaustion and then they feel the need to rest. They naturally stop doing anything that makes them tired. Yes, they do relax a bit, but only for a short spell. While recovering from extreme tiredness, their temporarily subdued stress starts catching up with them and they become highly strung up again.

It is quite clear that escaping from stress is never a good and lasting solution. Trying to understand the causes of stress seems to be the only sensible thing to do in such a situation.

Instead of fully understanding and coming to terms with the fact that they are boiling with animosity, a majority of the people suffering from stress bottle up their emotions; only a few show their strong feelings. When anger is restrained in this manner, these emotions begin to surface in the form of stress. Anger is an unpleasant emotion. Most often it manifests itself as resentment and ill will. Animosity, anger, and ill will are fundamentally the same. They all create stress.

Ill will exists whenever one harbours hostile, unkind or unfriendly feelings towards another human being. Once I noticed how there arose in me unfriendly attitudes and emotions when the recipient of a gift failed to send a written acknowledgement of the present that I had posted. The resentment festered for several weeks. What was the mistake I made? I was holding on to the sense of bitterness. I failed to see that unless I let go of it, I would continue to make my life a misery. How a small and unimportant matter had caused discontent! But once I released my grip on this feeling of dissatisfaction, the mind returned to normal. Simply *seeing* my silly situation was what helped me to restore calm. If one succeeds in seeing how the virus of unfriendliness results in unhappiness, that very insight is enough to drop ill will. It is as easy as that. When ill will is no more, the pleasant and serene state of goodwill arises of its own accord.

Any form of ill will begins to gnaw away at one's peace of mind not only throughout the day, but also during the night, for hate-based dreams can be horrible. Then sound sleep is not at all possible, and insufficient sleep, needless to say, has an adverse effect on health.

Hideous indeed are the faces of people saturated with hate. When human beings are plagued by ill will, their faces take on an unsightly expression. People with fierce tiger-like eyes are anything but attractive. I used to know a woman who was full of ill will, anger, and aggression. She had been quite beautiful when she was an adolescent girl. But the frustration of not finding a tolerable partner, let alone a caring husband, turned her into a person with a demonical appearance. Prospective partners and suitors were all turned off by the sight of her frightening features. Perhaps these men, after seeing her, sensed, and quite correctly too, that her troubled looks were an accurate reflection of her troubled mind.

Nowadays some men and women dye their hair,

undergo cosmetic surgery, wear make-up, adorn themselves with expensive or exotic jewellery, and do a thousand other things to beautify their faces and bodies. France is rightly famous for her haute-couture. But can anything cover up for long the hidden hate that lies within?

Nothing is uglier than a countenance distorted with ill will. Strong passions cannot be concealed easily nor trampled to death. Feelings of love or fear, for instance, are noticeable to the observant eye. In the same manner, feelings of animosity subtly surface in people's faces. They come into view in varying ways. A wry smile, a contemptuous glance, a dirty look or a raised voice are often telltale signs of spite and loathing.

There is another question that deserves careful consideration. If we hate someone now, and continue to do so instead of letting go of our lingering ill will, sooner or later the hated person will start hating us in return as well.

Those who sow the poisonous seeds of ill will cannot but reap the fruits of their misdeeds later. At some point in time, if not in the present, then in the unforeseeable future, the person who is currently teeming with ill will might well become the victim of somebody else's hate. It is not at all difficult to understand the workings of the universal law of karma.

14

NOTHING TO GAIN AND NOTHING TO LOSE

The sage Yogaswami (1872-1964) was famous for his spontaneous sayings. His casual comments were fortunately jotted down by some of his admirers, with the result that his remarkable utterances have become an important part of our sacred literature. The wisdom enshrined in his words is the priceless property he left behind for posterity. We are the lucky inheritors of his bequest. But we can benefit from it only to the extent that we succeed in understanding his mystical messages, and that is not easy.

I have found it difficult to make sense of his simple but profound statement that there is nothing to gain and nothing to lose. This aphorism can be interpreted in more ways than one, and we need to work out how to understand the hidden meanings behind it. Therefore, during the course of this talk, I would like to meditate on this question. Please bear with me as I discuss the practical implications of his advice that in life there is nothing to gain and nothing to lose.

Where had I been living before I took my first breath in this world? I do not know. Why was I born into this world? I had no say whatsoever in where I was going to be born. Even if I had had a say, I would probably have selected a better place. Surely, I would have chosen a celestial sphere with beings that aren't selfish, hateful, and violent. Is this world of ours a marvellous place despite our irrational attachment to it? The question is this: Have I gained anything spiritually by being born into this planet?

On the day of birth, I was unpretentious and uncorrupted by society. I was born fully naked. When I entered the world, I was devoid of the vanity of clothes, simple and unassuming, like the Jain ascetics of India. Without having any attachments, the Jain *munis* spend their days in a state of nothingness. Of what value are clothes? Clothes only help to cover up our bodies. What we wear can never conceal our hidden traits that are buried in the unexplored depths of our minds. There one can discover the malignant tendencies that we developed during our animalistic past stretching back to millions of years.

On that first day of life, I was a free human being. Yet, those responsible for my upbringing labelled me as a member of a certain caste. I was born into a so-called Buddhist society that practised the caste system according to which every member of society has to belong to a fixed social class that cannot be altered. What a betrayal of the Buddha's teachings! More than 2500 years ago, the Buddha vehemently denounced the Indian caste system. Let's not forget his well-known declaration that it is not by birth but by deeds and deeds alone that one becomes a Brahmin. Caste divisions have caused endless social conflicts. Are we sensitive to the pain and suffering of people belonging to the so-called low castes? Mahatma Gandhi called them Harijans—persons belonging to the god Vishnu. Out of deference to Gandhiji, the rest of society also started calling them Harijans. It was merely a change of name, there was no corresponding change of attitude towards these poor oppressed humans. There was certainly no change of heart, for this problem of caste discrimination continues to exist. So, in the manner of Yogaswami, we can say that there is nothing to gain by upholding the caste system.

When I was a child, my elders quite unnecessarily drilled into me that Buddhism was my religion. I was told that Buddhists were compassionate individuals who were overflowing with love, kindness, and generosity. As the years passed by, I realised that there were lots of non-Buddhists who were also full of compassion, loving-kindness, and generosity. These virtues can be found everywhere. By saying that Buddhists have a monopoly on virtue, my elders were creating deep divisions among the different religious groups that constitute society. Thank goodness, I am a student of comparative religion, which means that I am willing to learn from whoever is wise, liberated or enlightened, regardless of that person's religious background. Is there anything to be gained by hating other religions merely because you have committed yourself to one particular religion with its own dogmas, doctrines, and beliefs?

Once when I was a rebellious teenager, an uncle reminded me that I should call myself a Sinhalese.

"Be proud of the fact that ours is a noble Aryan race," he boasted.

"Uncle, what a stupid thing to say!" I retorted. "For me, there is only *one* race—the human race, consisting of all the men, women, and children in different parts of the globe. We *all* belong to that human race."

Believing that I had become a traitor to the Sinhala race, this uncle distanced himself from me for the rest of his life.

I maintain that races, unfortunately, exist because we are lacking in universal love. We may be educated and highly skilled, but even so, the spirit of brotherhood is somehow absent in our psychological make-up. We should ask ourselves: Is there anything to be gained by continuing to have these tribal barriers in our hearts?

In the expectation of having a *darshan* of Yogaswami and getting the saint's blessings, a certain middle-aged teacher from Jaffna town decided to go to Chundikuli where Yogaswami lived in a tiny *cadjan* hut. This devotee was not a bad man; his only shortcoming was that he harboured a deep detestation of the Sinhalese and their language. When the teacher entered the hut and prostrated himself on the ground before the saint in the customary manner, the holy man started speaking with him in Sinhalese instead of Tamil, which was the language that the two of them had in common! Sinhalese was the only language that Yogaswami used on that occasion, thus compelling the teacher to converse in the very language that he hated so much. The poor man was brought face to face with his racial hatred. In this way, he was made to deal with his problem, and thereby forced to find a solution to it. This incident may seem somewhat funny, but that was Yogaswami's medicine for treating the illness.

Let us look at the second part of Yogaswami's maxim: there is nothing to lose. In life, there are more disappointments than satisfaction. Naturally, we tend to think a lot about our sorrows. But if we dwell on our sad experiences, there is the risk of ending up as depressives. Yet, it is extremely important to face the fact that unhappiness is there. So, we have to take an impartial look at our unhappiness as a prelude to going beyond it once and for all. For example, a man or woman begins to feel miserable when experiencing unrequited love. The person you love fails to love you in return. What is one to do? What can one do to win over the heart of your beloved? If the other person has closed the door on the possibility of future friendship, one is compelled to resign oneself to that most unpleasant situation. When one stops holding on to one's frustration as a result of what had once happened, the mind regains its composure. Then, without a pang of regret, one can honestly say that there is nothing to lose, in the sense that one no longer suffers any feeling of deprivation.

When an investor is elated because he has succeeded in making a killing on the stock exchange or when a young student is in a triumphant mood because he has passed his exam with flying colours, both are full of the feeling that they have *gained* something. They are certainly not telling themselves that there is nothing to gain. They get a thrill out of a short-lived sense of achievement. But an excited mind, mind you, is a far cry from a calm one.

The serene mind is neither downcast nor delighted: it is in a placid, neutral condition. That supreme state of tranquillity comes into being after realising the truth that there is nothing to gain or lose. Not a thing disturbs the mind as it neither craves for anything nor suffers from any feeling of deprivation. That, I submit, was Yogaswami's inner state all the time. Although his emotions would swing, say when answering a question or when there is a devotional outpouring, most of the time he was peaceful, like the still waters of a lagoon.

A liberated sage's unselfishness and nobility of character spring from the fact that he or she is no longer enslaved by an ego. In what way is the mind of a liberated sage different from that of an ordinary unliberated human being? We function from a centre called the 'I' or the ego, whereas the liberated sage does not have this problem. The nature of the 'I' is the same in every unliberated person, but what constitutes the 'I' is different from individual to individual. My ego, for instance, is the product of all the conditioning influences that have made me what I am and shaped my outlook on life. Since my ego is different from yours, conflicts and misunderstandings between us are inevitable. It is not difficult to see, therefore, why this world is in a state of continuous confrontations.

Why did this man-made prison called the ego come into existence? There are many theories, but I think that this is how it happened and I shall try to explain its origins in the way I see it.

Our minds are whirlpools of thoughts and feelings. It is an unpleasant situation that creates a most unsettling sensation of insecurity. The thought process is in a state of perpetual flux, like a rapidly moving river that knows no stillness. Our longing for security is the soil in which the ego is born and in which it continues to thrive. This yearning to have an anchor of stability in the restless rapids of the mind results in the invention of a seemingly superior thought or entity that calls itself 'I'. In the fast moving and ever-changing thought processes, the artificially fabricated 'I', out of a desire for power and permanence, tries to control and order around the other thoughts. The illusory 'I', sensing the precariousness of its own existence, tries not only to prolong its life, but also to strengthen itself by acquiring things. Hence the unbridled greed to own this, that and the other. We can see why man's greed has become insatiable. It is understandable why capitalism is so popular today. Capitalism has spread to such an extent that even former communist states are gradually adopting capitalistic policies. This tendency is a question that baffles political and economic pundits. However, this matter is not a mystery to those who can clear-sightedly trace the roots of capitalism to the unquenchable avarice of man's ego.

If only we were intelligent enough to comprehend the origin of our urge to possess more and more. If only we knew that in truth, there is nothing to gain. In reality, the 'I' can never 'acquire' anything for the simple reason that the 'I' does not exist in the first place.

To survive in this world, we only need a minimum of possessions—a regular modest income, a roof over our head, some healthy food, and a few comfortable winter and summer clothes. You are probably familiar with Mahatma Gandhi's famous observation that although the world has enough for everyone's need, it hasn't enough for everyone's greed. We know those words are true, but we rarely take heed of them!

Our egos push us to obtain, both by fair means or foul, more and more of the things that the world has to offer. The extremely rich enjoy showing off their possessions—elegant and fashionable attire, palatial mansions, objets d'art, and so forth, hoping, thereby, to climb the social ladder and stand out in society. Money is valued not only for its own sake, but also because the sheer ownership of it makes one feel powerful. The affluent easily get to know important people; before long the wealthy and the ambitious find that they can even influence the policies of their governments. They soon become even more materialistic. Thereafter, there arises in them a certain pride and an indifference to spiritual values.

On his deathbed, it dawns on the millionaire that he cannot take away his fortune with him to the hereafter. With all his money and treasures, he suddenly realises that he cannot even buy ten additional minutes of life. All his belongings, he feels, have become utterly valueless. Great is his frustration as he breathes his last.

Perhaps some of you have had the experience of associating with at least a few extremely rich people. It so happened that in the course of my work, I was forced by circumstances to have dealings with several multimillionaires. I shouldn't mention their names of course. They were all different, but they had in common certain recognisable personality traits. That others were planning to steal their precious possessions from them was a fear that frequently lurked in their minds. So they became distrustful of everyone, including their genuine well-wishers. Their deepest fear was that even those closest and nearest to them had designs on what was theirs! One can never be sure if this fear was real or imaginary, especially in the case of Somerset Maugham (1874-1965). This well-heeled English novelist and short-story writer lived in a princely manner with many servants. Inside his posh villa in the south of France, he entertained the rich and the famous. Yet his brilliant mind was never free of the worry that his servants were helping themselves to his cash. What is the use of having sackfuls of gold if that makes you a miserable worrywart?

Take the case of a dying man with a spiritual bent. During his sojourn in our planet, he had been alert enough to spend his days with a sense of detachment from everything that the world has to offer and also from everyone. Since he never bothered *to gain* anything for himself, he now feels that as his frail body is sinking fast, he has nothing *to lose* either. As he passes away, those around his hospital bed notice on his face that elusive inner serenity. Interestingly, Buddhists believe that it is the purity or otherwise of one's last thought before death which determines *where* rebirth is going to take place. That last thought itself is determined by the *manner* in which a person has used his mind and behaved in life.

Farmers suffer severely when their crops fail as this leads to financial hardships; innocent victims of war often have to flee from their homelands and settle in foreign countries with cold climates; some students study hard and burn the midnight oil, yet they fail their examinations. Then we complain that life is full of injustices; we whine about the unfairness in the whole scheme of things. Some would say that we are only reaping the karmic results of our past misdeeds and negative thoughts. Can anyone be absolutely sure about why there is so much suffering in our lives?

Sometimes, however, I have found that in certain situations one can discover something that is positive in what had, at the beginning, seemed so very negative. In other words, what appears to be a large loss at first, turns out to be a great gain later. When one realises that the alarming negative factor has got cancelled out by the reassuring positive factor, what happens to the mind? The mind reverts to its primordial state of equilibrium. This feature is the hallmark of the silent mind, which is particularly noticeable in each and every spiritually liberated sage. In ordinary persons, however, it is less visible.

It is necessary to illustrate what has just been stated. When I was a youngster, I became heartbroken when I failed to pass the Senior School Certificate Examination. Those days, jumping over this hurdle signified the end of one's secondary education. Although I passed in all the subjects, I failed in Sinhalese, which was a compulsory subject. Sinhalese had always been my weakest subject. My lack of success left me feeling completely devastated.

It was then that a Buddhist monk came to my rescue. He carefully coached me, free of charge, and for the first time in my life, he taught me not only the rules of Sinhalese grammar, but also literary composition. I was also introduced to Buddhist philosophy as an additional bonus. After making a second attempt, I did pass this examination. In retrospect, I think my success was not an achievement worth mentioning, but I tremendously value the monk's lessons in philosophy. So, the traumatic event of failing the exam was actually a blessing in disguise in so far as what he taught helped to widen my horizons. We can see how a disaster can metamorphose into an immensely favourable outcome.

Now, I shall move on to another interesting story. On the evening of November 13 2015, a mass shooting took place at the Bataclan theatre in Paris. Terrorists shot dead

89 innocent victims who had gone there to enjoy a musical performance by the American band, Eagles Death Metal. Thereafter, the whole country was in a state of shock and mourning for several weeks.

Being a lover of that kind of entertainment, a young man, known to me, had travelled from the south of France, all the way to Paris at considerable expense, to be present at this special concert. But as he was feeling quite unwell on the evening of the musical show, he decided not to attend it. The thought of being away from this major event filled him with sadness. But because of his absence there that evening, the young man escaped being killed. Ironically, it was ill health that saved his life.

Some might think that it was probably his guardian angel's intervention—making him fall ill—that protected him from the jaws of death. Anyway, we can see that this person neither lost anything of great value nor gained anything that evening, for it was the operation of the law of karma that had determined his right to continue living.

Why did I come to this conclusion? I remember one of the four *Mahavakyas* (Great Sayings) of Yogaswami: *Eppavo Mudintha Karyam* (Long ago the event was completed). Long ago it was all over. Everything has been foreordained. We like to think that we can determine the course of our lives, and in a general sense, even influence the course of human affairs. Does it not feed our vanity to believe that we have the faculty to form the future? But man is only an insignificant instrument in the hands of the Absolute, which alone is in charge of the past, present, and future. A self-centred man prides himself on the view that he has free will, when in reality he is only a mere puppet in the hands of a hidden power. We had better understand this truth and surrender ourselves to the Absolute. The Absolute is not necessarily a being. It is probably an invisible energy in the universe that determines everything.

An address to the Siva Nandi Foundation in
Paris on 27 April, 2016

15

FEAR OF
FALLING ILL

For years I have been haunted by the fear of falling sick. I have known many persons, friends, relations, schoolmates, and colleagues, who have suffered from various illnesses. Long is the list of terrible diseases and minor ailments that have troubled them. Naturally, a certain uneasy feeling prevailed that it was only a matter of time before I also became indisposed in the wake of any major crisis.

Several times during my childhood, I was down with malaria. Once, the attack was so severe that I had fits of delirium. It will be difficult to find in Sri Lanka anyone from my generation who has not fallen victim to either malaria, typhoid or dysentery. Being seriously ill was the norm; being the picture of health all the time was the exception. Those days, none would dare to fault a person who absents himself from school or work due to bad health. It is not difficult, therefore, to understand why the fear of falling ill continues to exist.

Is not the fear of falling ill a sort of warning as it alerts one to the importance of never neglecting one's body? I venture an opinion that the fear of falling ill is a most useful emotion, in so far as it spurs people on to ensure that their immune systems are kept as strong as possible. Thereby, the body is helped to protect itself from various diseases.

My motto has long been 'mens sana in corpore sano': a sound mind in a sound body. One of the most valuable gifts that the ancient *rishis* of India bestowed on the world is the system of *hatha* yoga. Based on their knowledge of the workings of the human body, they prescribed certain *asanas* (yogic postures) and *pranayama* (yogic breathing practices) to tone up the body and oxygenate it respectively. Yoga regenerates the entire body, especially the cells and the nerves. Without having the firm foundation of yoga, it is difficult to launch into spirituality. But spirituality, let us be very clear about it, is not the preserve of yoga-orientated men and women. Anyone can start leading the spiritual life, be he for yoga or opposed to it or be he healthy or suffering from an illness. However, those who are in poor shape might not have the time, energy, stamina or even the incentive to give their undivided attention to spirituality. So, it is a great advantage to be fully fit in body before setting out on otherworldly pursuits.

In the little masterpiece of a book called *At the Feet of the Master*, written by J. Krishnamurti when he was a little boy, he likens the body to a horse upon which one rides. This horse has to be treated well. One has to take good care of it;

one should not overwork it. It has to be fed only pure food and drink, and it must also be kept clean, without even the minutest speck of dirt. Without a perfectly clean and healthy body, says Krishnamurti, neither is one capable of doing the arduous work of spiritual preparation nor can one bear the endless strain entailed in that task.

There must be many whose loving care of their bodies far exceeds that of mine. Anyway, I shall briefly describe the things I do to make sure that my ageing body—is there anyone whose body does not age?—stays strong, supple and healthy.

It is absolutely necessary to have at least one bowel movement per day. A sea of troubles will be in store if the system gets clogged up with toxic waste.

"Don't come to school if your bowels haven't been emptied," a teacher used to advise us. People those days were less squeamish than what they are today and they discussed such subjects openly. The constipated should make sure that they eat more vegetables, fruits, grains, and foods with a lot of roughage. Apples, figs, and prunes aid elimination. A lot of physical activities such as walking and gardening are necessary for persons who have to do sedentary jobs.

To have an immune system that can resist negative forces such as pollution that diminish its power, one can begin the day by drinking a glassful of lemon juice. The juice should be mixed with clean water, spring water preferably, and swallowed slowly in the form of small mouthfuls. Since heat destroys the Vitamin C present in the valuable juice, it is best to use either cold or slightly warm water. To protect the teeth's enamel from acid corrosion, one should remember to brush them with toothpaste immediately after drinking the lemon juice.

As far as possible, we try to eat only organically grown whole grains, fruits, and vegetables. How dangerous it is to consume contaminated non-organically produced foods! It is imprudent to take agricultural foods wherein even small amounts of insecticides, pesticides or herbicides have gone into their production. Those who allow their poor bodies to become poisoned by eating these polluted products, sooner or later become prone to different kinds of deadly diseases. It is far better to live on a small quantity of pure food than on a large quantity of inferior fare. What matters is not quantity but quality.

At one time, as much from habit as from craving, I used to take tea or coffee whenever I felt tired. Later on, realising that fatigue can be caused either by an inadequate intake of water or insufficient periods of rest, I stopped taking these popular beverages. A lack of water can cause dehydration whereas an excess of it could result in high blood pressure. Through trial and error, I have been able to find a balance. In toto, I require about two litres of liquids per day. The amount of liquid required is different for each individual.

I am sick and tired of hearing people in France, which is one of the leading wine producing nations, praise the supposed health benefits of taking some wine. They drink it with relish, doing so either before, during or after their meals. How they rationalise their behaviour so that what they do somehow does not seem bad, even though there is abundant medical evidence that alcohol has a deleterious effect on the liver! Besides, is an intoxicated mind capable of seeing things exactly as they are? Not surprisingly, in some religious traditions, the consumption of alcohol is taboo. It is better to face the world as it is with all its unpleasantness and suffering, instead of temporarily escaping from it by means of the bottle. When spirits enter our body the less spiritual we become. Is a tipsy mind capable of clarity of vision?

I have heard it said that a human being can live for lengthy periods without solid food, but none can last long without water. Water is indispensable for survival. Decades ago, well water was potable in many Asian countries. Today, however, because of the rapid growth in numbers, there is hardly a country in Asia that is not overpopulated. In India, for example, the habitable areas are fast diminishing. Consequently, the water in some parts is unreliable; there is widespread faecal pollution. From personal experience, I know that even bottled water is not hundred per cent pure. One has to boil water for a prescribed period of time to make sure that it is safe. In France, tap water is excessively chlorinated. We try to purify our tap water by introducing powdered clay into it, but I realise that this might not be a foolproof way of preventing pollution.

Before allowing food to pass down the throat, it should be thoroughly masticated and swirled around in the mouth.

This cannot be done if one has to hurry a meal. The digestive system can easily handle only slowly-masticated food. Why strain the digestive organs by introducing into them inadequately ground food? Whenever possible, I try to avoid eating food that is glutinous, fatty or salty.

During the rainy period or when it is too cold, we are forced to have our meals indoors, but when the weather becomes warm, we eat in the comfortable shade of a tree in the garden. It is usually under a spreading tree with pine needles. The birds entertain us with their cheerful chirps and songs. There are times though, when these feathered friends annoy us with their droppings.

To save time, many who are stressed have gotten into the bad habit of skipping their breakfast. But as regards those who have wisely decided to have breakfast, it is sadly more likely to be a snack than a proper meal, consisting mostly of two or three buttery croissants and a cup of strong coffee that is quickly gulped down. We are an exception. For us, breakfast is the main meal of the day.

We begin with a dish of at least five different fruits; fruits that are in season have priority. Some health care workers call it the 'anti-cancer diet'. I do not know why they concluded that such a combination of fruits combat this dreaded illness. Anyway, we do concur with their conclusion. There are other items in this dish of fruits such as nuts. Thereafter, we eat muesli with grated apples, ginger, soya milk, and a large spoonful of molasses. To this mixture are added some pumpkin seeds and raisins.

With our tummies so full of the sumptuous breakfast, there is usually no great craving for a heavy meal at lunchtime, which is taken in the early afternoon. Our light lunch is normally a simple salad. Its composition depends on what is available in the market. Claudia prepares it with leaves of medicinal value from our garden—parsley, mint or rocket. Occasionally, we use lettuce from the market as it is difficult to grow it in our dry Mediterranean climate. For dessert, we enjoy soya yogurt, cheese, bananas or mangoes. An hour or two following sunset, we have an early dinner. It is a modest meal of boiled rice with one or two curried vegetables. Often, there is a slightly spiced dish of red lentils. We attach great importance to getting the right nutrition. Many do think we are crazy.

"Yours is a food house," remarked a neighbour with an amused expression. She was not wrong. I believe that unless we take a passionate interest in finding what the right food is, and then follow it up by strictly consuming that and that alone, one runs the risk of falling ill.

Why eat things that catch one's fancy? How easily we are swayed by advertisements in newspapers and television! But those who are keen on being sound as a bell should be guided by their well-informed minds, not by the cravings and dictates of their greedy tongues.

Despite all of one's well-planned efforts to avoid illness, there is absolutely no guarantee whatsoever that we are not going to contract a disease sooner or later. Yet one's practical efforts to avoid illness would at least diminish, if not altogether eliminate, this lurking fear of falling ill. That is something.

There was a time in my life when I liked brief sojourns into Indian ashrams where I did meet interesting people who were knowledgeable about spiritual teachings and practices. I remember having conversations with *yogis* and ascetic seekers who were indifferent to what they ate, provided it was vegetarian. Whether their food was going to be beneficial or harmful to their health was a question that did not interest them whatsoever. So, they did not mind taking inferior food, even stale or rotten things to eat, so long as what entered their bodies quickly helped to assuage their hunger. Having such an attitude to food was seen by them as a sure sign of their spirituality! Some of the *yogis* who resided in the ashrams were so feeble that they talked hesitatingly and walked haltingly. Severely punishing the body was viewed as a virtue. They took pride in their austerity. Little did they realise that pride in any form was the very antithesis of spirituality.

In the course of life, one tends to fall ill, not just once but several times. So, sicknesses can be correctly seen as passing events. Every illness, be it serious or otherwise, could eventually result in one's own demise and there is the rub. In other words, the fear of dying *inheres* in the fear of falling ill. Let us examine if the fear of dying is rational or irrational.

The fondest aspiration of every Muslim is to go to Paradise, but is there any guarantee that it would happen?

Catholics believe that after death they end up as residents of Hell, Purgatory or Heaven. But does any Catholic know with certainty what exactly is in store for him or her after death? Hindus and Buddhists believe that where they are going to be reborn will be determined by their past karma. But do they have a say in where they are going to be reborn? Is the matter negotiable?

Since we cannot control or direct what is going to take place after death, what is the best thing to do? What, in other words, is the sensible course of action to take? Why not forget this question altogether and consequently be at peace with ourselves? One has to resign oneself to the fact that human beings are not immortal.

A good student works hard in preparation for a forthcoming examination. Being success-orientated, he naturally burns the midnight oil, never allowing his single-minded determination to waver in any way. Yet, after the exam is over, it is not within his power to do anything that would ensure a favourable outcome. After having done his best at the examination hall, all he can now do is to sit back and hope for a positive result. Similarly, can anyone be certain that he is never going to fall ill? All that the intelligent can do is to leave no stone unturned in the search for perfect health, then simply sit back and hope that the body never breaks down.

Although the prudent attach great importance to good health, our enthusiasm for it might well result in a certain state of continuously worrying about it, for we might often think about the various dos and don'ts, and end up as hypochondriacs, who imagine that they suffer from this, that and the other even while being in fine fettle. Being mentally alert at all times will prevent the occurrence of imagined maladies. Eternal vigilance is truly the very essence of meditation.

16

FEAR OF
DEATH

It is rather presumptuous of me to write about death. Since I have no first-hand experience of death, the truth is that I know next to nothing about the subject. Philosophers and religious writers have only thought and speculated about death and the hereafter. I agree with those critics who say that one should, first of all, have *personal* experience of death. Therefore, some writers who eagerly want to write about this important issue do not dare to venture their opinions.

In previous lives—if there is such a process as the *samsaric* cycle of births and deaths—I would have had the experience of dying, but in my present life I have no recollection whatsoever of my former births and deaths. Has anyone met a person who, having died, comes back to give details of the experience of death? Interestingly, Shakespeare described death as "the undiscovered country from whose bourn no traveller returns."

Death is something that is difficult to imagine. I imagine death as a sort of occurrence that is similar to being unconscious, perhaps like having a total blackout during a surgical operation under the influence of general anaesthesia. I once asked a surgeon whether the mind is active during a general anaesthetic. She answered that her patients' image-making process continues while they are on the operating table. In that case, one wonders if the death experience can be likened to what happens during a coma, assuming it to be an imageless state. Is death like being in a deep sleep state wherein the image-making process has fallen into abeyance? One does not know with any degree of certainty what actually happens at death. For this reason, the domain of death has become a fertile field for fiction writers.

There is evidence that the thought process does continue even after the brain has ceased to function: the mind continues to have a life of its own even after one has passed away.

Today, there is a fairly large and growing literature on Near Death Experience or NDE. But these accounts, fascinating though they are for us, are only the outpourings of people on the *verge* of death. We are still in the dark as regards the death experience per se.

Throughout this discussion, the word 'death' is used to refer to the state when a person is brain dead: the brain no longer works in the normal way; more correctly expressed, the brain no longer works in any way at all. Only the mind operates. This form of demise is often called 'clinical death'.

It is an inescapable fact that we *do* fear death, despite our failure to understand its nature completely. All living creatures are afraid of it; our feelings of uncertainty and insecurity aggravate the fear. Would not this fear disappear without a trace the day we fully comprehend death?

In a sense, man's struggle to survive springs from this primordial fear of death. We have many fears, such as the fear of becoming homeless, the fear of losing one's source of income, the fear of having a tragic accident on the road, the fear of running afoul of the law and so forth. Of all the fears we harbour, the fear of extinction is the strongest; all other fears seem to be tied to this basic fear of death.

Some might argue that it is good and salutary to have this fear of death. For if this were absent, would there not be the possibility of our becoming neglectful of our health and well-being? Would we then not easily succumb to illness and risk death? If people willingly give in to death, would not the human species soon disappear? Yes, it might happen. Yet many might disagree. Given the unpleasant situation arising from the fact that it is almost impossible to change human nature, those with a deep distrust of human beings might surmise that it will not be a great loss if homo sapiens were to vanish off the face of the earth. Being cynical about human nature, they will never regret if someday human beings cease to exist. They would surely ask, "Are we so wonderful and marvellous that we deserve to exist?"

Rare is the individual in whom the fear of death is not present. In this connection, it is necessary to refer to the apparent fearlessness of Socrates in the face of death. Generally viewed throughout the centuries as one of the principal founders of Western philosophy, Socrates had been condemned to death—he was required to drink the poisonous hemlock. Before passing away, Socrates spoke his last words to Crito. "Crito," he said, "we owe a rooster to Asclepius. Do not forget this debt."

Before we leave this world, must we not clear our debts and die peacefully with a clear conscience in the manner of this sage?

In ancient Greece, Asclepius was the god for curing illnesses. So Socrates does his moral duty to the deity before his life comes to an end. After turning down Crito's suggestion that he should try to escape from prison, Socrates decided to take the toxic mixture. The great thinker was offering himself as a sacrifice to the god, probably because he believed that such a deed might please the deity. At the same time, he was, as it were, atoning for the sins, moral failings, and misfortunes of Athens. He had been a critic of Athens at the time when the city-state was in decline. In addition, Socrates held the view that no genuine philosopher fears death.

Discussions about death evoke in me memories of the pain and suffering experienced by my parents during the last few years of their lives. Both of them found the strains of their severe illnesses unbearable. Therefore, they seemed to be looking forward to their day of departure from this world. For many years, my father had been becoming physically weaker and weaker. He suffered from chronic arthritis, but he died of pneumonia. My mother, who had chronic asthma, also passed away in agony; it happened while she was having a severe asthmatic attack. Some of those who attended my mother's funeral remarked that there was a serene expression on her face as she lay motionless in her coffin. With such words were they trying to console those of us who were bereaved? No, they were complimenting my deceased mother on her virtuous character.

Several years later, at my father's funeral, his face also looked very calm. Both faces had a look of being greatly relieved, so pleased to leave this world wherein they had been through trying times. As they were shuffling off their mortal coils, did my parents have any foreknowledge of their hereafter? If there is such a thing as life after death, who knows if my parents are happy or unhappy in their new abodes?

At the two funerals of my parents, it was the women folk, clad in white mourning saris, who wailed. Some of the men folk had a solemn expression, but on the whole, the men did not outwardly show their emotions. Why did I remain calm? I was composed because of my deep understanding of the Buddhist doctrine of *anicca*: the essential impermanence of everything. I was already familiar with this teaching. Deep was my conviction that the *anicca* doctrine is part of the eternal verities of life. According to this doctrine, everything is transitory; everything is in a state of flux. Nothing lasts forever. Every living thing must sooner or later pass away. It is unrealistic to think that life in any form is going to have a permanent existence. Comprehending this great truth enables one to accept death philosophically.

Before looking at the outside world, one has only to turn inwards and observe how our very minds change all the time like quicksilver. Our minds are never still because of their essential mercurial character. One fleeting thought is immediately followed by another short-lived one. This rapid process goes on and on endlessly. Ceaseless change is the norm. Life is recurrent and so is death.

Any alert individual can see how the workings of Mother Nature illustrate the principle of *anicca* or impermanence. Every changing season has its own charm. However, each one lasts only for a short time, usually three months, and then a new season begins. Change is part of the natural order of things. Marvellous are the various shades of autumn colours that one can see and savour while enjoying walks in leafy woods and parks, trudging through scattered heaps of lovely fallen leaves.

Why be crestfallen when trees start shedding their leaves? Cheer up! Soon the splendid spring will come and beautiful new leaves will appear on the bare branches. A great renewal is set in motion. Nature will burst with new life all over again. Death is never an everlasting end, but simply a sign of a new beginning.

Hindus and Buddhists believe that their present life is just one episode in a long series of reincarnations. They, therefore, do not kill themselves in despair when someone near and dear passes away or when they are in the throes of a terrible personal crisis. Though they can never again see the faces of their dear departed ones, they sincerely hope that all the deceased are more prosperous and happier now than ever before in their new surroundings, wherever that might be.

Not every dying person passes away in an agitated state. For example, Dr. E. W. Adikaram, a saintly man and a lifelong friend of mine, was a scholar, an educationist, and a deeply religious man who died peacefully in his sleep. Except for his few personal effects, he did not own anything else. Without a pang of regret, he withdrew from the world with dignity and a great sense of detachment.

Spiritually advanced souls sometimes breathe their last in this way. They often have a premonition that they will soon have to face their end. A short time before his death, Krishnamurti spoke to a close friend of his about it, even giving details about the date and place of his imminent demise.

We know without a shadow of a doubt that every living being will someday have to say a final goodbye to life. Is there anything one can do to diminish the sorrow and the fear of death? This matter merits consideration. Death being a blow, even a shattering blow, is there anything that can be done to soften the blow?

Realising the importance of having a mind that is like an empty suitcase, not a heavy one, when going away for good and leaving, once and for all, the house of life, one can begin to get rid of every burdensome item, not just when one is on the verge of leaving oneself for good on one's deathbed, but right *now*. For no one knows when death is going to knock on the door. If the dying person begs and asks, "Please wait for a few more days", is death going to agree to such a request?

It is necessary to reiterate the importance of meeting one's legal and moral obligations. Have I done all my worldly duties? If so, I will neither burden other people with such problems nor will unfinished business trouble me when I am dying. Have I made my last will and testament? Have I given away all my possessions? Have I made provisions for my spouse and children, if any? A friend of mine remembered to pay all his funeral expenses before dying; another friend bequeathed his corpse to the cause of medical and scientific research, including transplant surgery.

Giving away one's material possessions can be quite easy, especially when one is no longer attached to them. But if a man treasures his goods, it is with reluctance that he would part with what belongs to him. He would probably have an inner struggle if he decides to donate them to any person or organisation. Only when he ceases to cling to the things which he owns will he be ready to offer them with a pure heart to those in need.

Potters take pride in the beautiful objets d'art that they make out of clay. Highly qualified academics are more than pleased with their university degrees. Parents are proud of the achievements of their offspring. When politicians win the elections, they start having swollen heads, which, in turn, results in their soon forgetting all the election promises they made to the electors. All prize winners' self-esteem, which is a respectable form of pride, tends to increase on receiving their awards. Their egos receive a boost. Do all these categories of people see the long-lasting psychological damage resulting from pride? Why not drop pride in the same way that a pot falls down and breaks into tiny pieces?

All our lives, alas, we have been burdened by our psychological luggage. We have seen that one such piece of luggage is pride; jealousy is yet another item. Jealousy can gnaw at the mind and disturb our peace of mind. Let us discard this item also well before we go the way of all flesh.

Let go of animus and anger. Let not our hate for various people who have harmed us in the past come back to haunt us at the eleventh hour of our lives. If we can do this, the fear of death could become a thing of the past.

We have so far considered only a few of our most glaring traits. It is well beyond the scope of this modest essay to examine all the negative traits of man. Long will be the list of all the characteristics that constitute our dark side! It is up to each and every individual to explore his psyche. First of all, let us wait until each of our traits surfaces. Let us notice their existence and then look at them impartially and non-judgementally until they fully unfold themselves. If we have gone thus far, the traits will simply drop one by one effortlessly. Sometimes, they can all drop at the same time, but that takes place very rarely.

Then one comes by an aching void; it defies description. Actually, Pure Consciousness was always there, but we have been covering it up by means of thought and by running away from it most of the time. Let us try to live in this state instead of everlastingly avoiding it.

What exactly is the void? When the mind has been cleansed of all that is negative, the void comes into being. For the want of a suitable word, we call it emptiness or nothingness.

The liberated person uses thought only to communicate with others; thought is his servant, never his master. He knows when to use thought and when not to use it, for when thought is wrongly used it distorts perception.

Pure Consciousness is our natural state until the mind blocked its operation. It is the state of spiritual purity, our very inescapable essence. All the thoughts, words, and deeds of the liberated spring from Pure Consciousness. In this unconditioned realm, the flower of compassion suddenly blooms. Such an exalted being finds that he naturally has all the virtues. He never has to struggle to become virtuous. He is no longer in the world of becoming, but in the world of *Being*.

Life will run its course and come to a natural end. Shortly thereafter, one is either reborn in a celestial sphere or not reborn at all. The liberated ones, the *jivanmuktas*, are no longer caught in the cycle of births and deaths.

17

BRUSH WITH
DEATH

Most impressive is the beauty of the golden statue of the standing Madonna which is right atop the massive structure of Notre Dame de la Garde. The basilica is situated on the highest point in Marseille, which is the southernmost of the important French cities. The basilica dominates the city's skyline. On arrival at the railway station, I cannot help gazing at it before walking down its long flight of stairs.

The basilica is our favourite haunt whenever we visit this teeming port. We love going to Marseille once a fortnight. We sympathise with the homeless who sit on the pavements and beg for provisions. Many of them are political or religious refugees who have fled to France from life-threatening situations in their war-torn countries.

Despite the fact that I was born and raised in the Buddhist tradition and educated mostly in Buddhist institutions, for unknown reasons I have always been strangely drawn to the Virgin Mary. This attraction is probably ascribable to Our

Lady's purity of character. It is clear in my mind that this love and respect does not originate from the desire to gain any material or spiritual benefit. I have always believed that devotion should be devoid of any motive whatsoever. Only purposeless devotion deserves to be called pure devotion. Fortunately, my devotion to the Virgin Mary is of this kind. It is necessary to stress this point because nowadays the vast majority worship Our Lady with an ulterior motive. Not surprisingly, she is often known as Our Lady of Perpetual Succour. They sincerely believe that she gives help and sympathy to those in need. Although there is substance to that belief, it always seemed so small-minded that so many follow her merely because of her usefulness to them for the purpose of dealing with the vicissitudes of life.

The best lover is the man or woman who loves for the sheer joy of loving without wanting anything back in return.

Whenever we visit the small, sparsely decorated crypt of Notre Dame de la Garde, we sit there quietly for about twenty minutes. During this short spell, we unwind the mind while meditating in silence. The heart is cleansed and the spirit activated. As we leave the place, we feel ready once again to remain uninfluenced by the corrupt and wayward ways of the world.

Throughout the year, tourists would frequent this mountain top to see the beautiful basilica's interior and enjoy the excellent scenery outside. They can get a panoramic view of the great city and its environs, including the harbour. On taking in the vast expanse of the deep blue waters of the

Mediterranean below and the immense blue sky above, one becomes aware of the endlessness and the limitlessness of space. One can get a glimpse of the infinite.

The golden statue of the Virgin gleams in the sun. Stunning is its brilliance. Simply seeing that statue over and over again tires neither the eyes nor the mind. Desiring to enjoy its sight is often my reason for going to Marseille.

We use the French railways mostly for travelling to Marseille. When the weather is fine, we like to take the train to the seaside resort of Saint Raphael where we dip several times in the sea, wade through the water, and go for long walks along the soft sandy beach. About once a year, we go by train to Switzerland to meet with Claudia's relations who live in Bern.

On one occasion, after spending a few days in the Swiss city of Winterthur, we returned by train to Les Arcs-sur-Argens where we live. What a relief it was to be back home! But we felt fatigued after this long and arduous journey of nearly seven hours. Our entire luggage was in two trolleys. Claudia was walking ahead of me with her trolley and I was following her with mine, which, like hers, was also heavy with books, clothes, and shoes.

At the Les Arcs-sur-Argens railway station, passengers are required to walk along a descending staircase before they move towards the exit. I took Claudia's trolley also. Without loosening my grip on the two trolleys, I was pushing them down the slope next to the steps. The sheer weight of the trolleys pushed me down with the result that my whole body jerked forwards. I continued to slip on several steps before reaching the landing. It was then that my head dashed against the wall. It was like a heavy blow to the head. I collapsed on the floor and blacked out.

On regaining consciousness, I remember Claudia's voice. "Are you all right?" she asked.

I tried to say something, but soon I realised that I had lost the power of speech. My lips moved, but the words failed to come out. When I tried to stand up, my arms and legs would not move at all. I wanted to lift up my legs again, but I found them lifeless. I heard someone say in a male voice that he had called an ambulance and it was on its way. I wondered if I was paralysed from the waist down as a result of this accident. The thought of spending the rest of my life in a wheelchair was absolutely horrifying. That possibility came as a great shock. In addition, it occurred to me that I was on the verge of passing away any moment. Wanting to dispel these dreadful thoughts, I closed my eyes.

A few minutes passed and I was still awake, though in a dazed condition. Suddenly, a vivid picture of the Madonna flashed through my mind. That beautiful image bore some resemblance to her statue at Notre Dame de la Garde. I was so cheered up by what I had seen that I felt that the worst was over. When I opened my eyes, I noticed a few strangers standing around me, staring at me with curiosity as I was lying supine on the floor. Then I realised that I was suddenly able to rise to my feet as though nothing had happened.

When the ambulance staff arrived, they insisted on carrying me on a stretcher to the nearest hospital. I was rushed to the emergency section of the hospital in Draguignan. My whole body was X-rayed and I was told that not a single bone had been broken. Needless to say, I am extremely grateful for Our Lady's assistance. It was a remarkable recovery. She did me a favour.

On second thoughts, I wonder if it was such a favour. Although she did spring to my assistance at my hour of need, was it not my stock of good karma that really enabled me to rise from the cold cement floor where, being unable to move, my body had been motionlessly lying flat? Karmically speaking, I was deserving of help. Had I been unworthy of it, would she have intervened in this critical situation?

Among her other roles, I regard the Virgin Mary as an executive arm of the karmic law that operates in the entire universe. It is like this: The Blessed Virgin is analogous to my post woman who regularly delivers a letter containing a cheque. This cheque comes from my bank wherein is kept all my hard-earned money over the years. That fund is my good karma. While I am deeply appreciative of all the services provided by the efficient post woman, I realise that I will continue to receive such cheques in the future *only* if I ensure that I always have a good bank balance. What will always stand us in good stead is not the blessing of a celestial being or a 'Saviour', but our good karma.

18

UNWIND AND FIND PEACE OF MIND

As usual, I got out of bed exactly at 6 a.m. I never set an alarm clock to wake me up at that time. Rising this way is involuntary. That morning, I simply found it uncomfortable to continue lying on my bed although it was warm and cosy. Being up early is a good habit that developed over a lifetime. I can trace it back to my boyhood when I used to wake up at 4 a.m. to study for at least two hours before making a dash to school. Those days, I had to ride a bicycle and snake my way through congested streets to be in time for the classes. There are good habits and bad habits. There is really no need to have a lie-in unless one is feeling quite inert or otherwise indisposed. Some mornings are stormy, such as when the mistral is in full swing, and some are windy, pitch-dark or freezing cold. But always at 6 a.m. I am up, come what may.

On this dark and chilly morning, the amber-coloured streetlights looked hazy. The fog diffused the yellowish brown lustre, making it difficult to see the long green hedge, the tall pines, the olive trees, and the unmown lawn. Our garden took on an attractive golden hue. All these passing changes in appearance were compensation enough for a great loss—the morning star in all its sparkling and silvery splendour was not visible. On clear and cloudless days, its dazzling rays are a source of inspiration.

As I opened the doors and windows of the house and put all the bedding and night clothes on the balcony for an airing, I heard the noises of the dustmen. They were removing waste from wheeled dustbins. I surmised that these workmen were toiling away at their daily rounds of garbage collecting. They were in too much of a hurry, they were anything but relaxed. Theirs was the task of rushing behind a moving lorry. All at once, the calm of the dawn was disturbed when one man loudly banged a dustbin on a wrought iron gate. "Merde!" he screamed.

Having heard that expletive so many times, it fell flat. I wasn't upset in the least. I heard a neighbour revving up his engine very loudly before driving his car to work. This daily ritual was enough to wake up the whole household. I wondered if he had cared to do a few physical exercises and enjoy a quiet breakfast before leaving home. Nowadays, most people begin the day with a cup of coffee. I used to do that a long time ago, but I gave up coffee. I feared that any artificial stimulant of that kind might shock the system and strain the heart. My poor neighbour had to race to his workplace at the crack of dawn. Six times a week he was obliged to do this as a matter of routine. Hélas! I could have shrugged my shoulders, as the French do, and cried out, "c'est la vie!—that's life!"

I felt the need to go to the toilet. This bodily urge arises as regularly as clockwork. Fortunately for me, the eliminative organs have been trained to function at set times. Many years ago, I remember how our thoughtful kindergarten teacher, an English lady, asked all her pupils to carry out this instruction: "Begin your day only after emptying your bowels. Don't go to school if your bowels haven't moved. Once you're clean, you'll be ready to face the world." Wearing spotless clothes wasn't good enough those days unless one also cared to clean up within. It is worth mentioning that our science teacher told us that the squatting position was the best as it was conducive to complete evacuation. Many animals know this posture intuitively.

In France, there is a deplorable lack of public conveniences. This unfortunate situation should be rectified as it is a great danger to public health. We are all concerned about keeping the environment clean. However, only a few realise that faecal pollution can cause a whole host of diseases. If contaminated water seeps below the ground, where there is an abundant supply of water, which is termed the water table, thousands could perish. Many might dismiss this matter, saying that such a nightmarish scenario is only a mere theoretical possibility. The environmental catastrophes that take place in the Third World can also happen in Europe. Treating water with various chemicals is not the best solution. The chemicals used can become dangerous to human beings. First of all, we'd better avoid fouling the earth. That might lessen the need to depend on chemicals. The natural beauty and cleanliness of France is marred by the inadequacy of public conveniences. Something must be done if France wants to continue being one of the leading tourist destinations in the world.

Throughout the centuries, one of the distinguishing features of French culture has been the great importance given to beauty and art. The appreciation of beauty in all its forms is deeply ingrained in the French psyche. Given that aesthetic considerations are part and parcel of their outlook on life, is it aesthetically pleasant when toilets in public places and trains are, more often than not, disorderly, unclean, and revolting to the sight and smell? They are poorly maintained and fail to flush.

Once, while browsing around in Shakespeare and Company, the famous English bookshop in Paris, I had an interesting conversation with a fellow bibliophile, an elderly American professor from Los Angeles. He took me out to a nearby cafe for some refreshments. While I sipped green tea, he gulped down several pints of beer. Afterwards, as we were strolling in a little park in the city, he remarked that the absence of toilets was a clever device to force visitors to go to restaurants. He told me that he wanted to pass water then and there, although he knew that answering calls of nature in public was an offence. Casting caution to the winds, the learned scholar decided to take the law into his own hands. After unzipping his tweed trousers, he waited impatiently for a suitable moment when there were no passersby; and when none were around, he quietly went behind a bush. It was there, lo and behold, that the American tourist saw a uniformed policeman, who, puffing his cigarette, was urinating!

"Bonjour!" exclaimed the brazen cop.

"Vive la France!" declared the carefree American. "This is surely the land of liberté!"

That autumn morning on my balcony, I was still saddened by the news I had received the previous night. Marie-Magdalene, a long-time friend of ours in Nice, had telephoned to say that she had been diagnosed with colon cancer. For years she had found it difficult to defecate. I was tired of trying to persuade her to become a vegetarian. Although she eventually did become a semi-vegetarian by eating lots of fruits and vegetables, Marie-Magdalene continued to take seafood and steak in abundance. In addition, she did not stop her addiction to tobacco, much to her husband's displeasure. Once, I ran into her on the platform of a railway station. She had been reading an article in Le Monde and puffing a cigarette with relish.

"Try one and enjoy it," she had said with a smile, offering me a fag. "It's from a plant and an excellent vegetarian product." She loved to tease people.

I felt a pang of remorse for having forgotten over the years to teach Marie-Magdalene a wonderful yogic exercise that would surely have helped to rectify her intestinal condition. I had been a part-time yoga teacher in Australia.

Whenever a student had complained of having a stomach ache or poor digestion, I would show the sufferer how to do *Uddiyana Bandha.* This exercise involves the complete control of the stomach muscles. One has to suck in the muscles as far inwards as possible, thus forming an abdominal cavity. It is necessary to hold and retain this lock as long as possible without breathing. Those who care to do this exercise every morning on an empty stomach will reap many benefits, including the toning up of the abdominal organs.

It was about 7 o'clock and there was only a luminous patch of crimson in the grey skies. The bright yellow autumn leaves in a neighbouring garden stood out against the semi-darkness of the morn. In our garden, the Lagerstroemia tree with its red leaves and the roses in shades of red and pink beautified the place. All the roses were in full bloom and a few bees were buzzing around. Although we grow several kinds of fruit trees, only the orange-coloured and delicious persimmon fruits and the rich red fruits of the strawberry tree were in season. Savouring the fragrant flowers and tasty fruits of the garden helped to counter a certain feeling of sadness in this melancholy month when the leaves begin to fall and warn one of the icy-cold days that are yet to come. Several enchanting magpies, long-tailed with lustrous black-and-white plumage, hopped in the garden and moved around. They seemed to be full of a certain ceaseless curiosity. Quite a number of local pigeons were perched on the branches of the pine trees. All these birds that turn up at this time were impatiently waiting for their breakfast.

Claudia loves to feed her feathered friends. So she places a small quantity of various grains on an elevated slab, beside a watering trough. The leftovers from the kitchen are also offered in this way. Once she has scattered their fare on the slab, the birds scramble for some morsels. Sometimes they flutter their wings and make a big noise while struggling and fighting for their food. Immediately after they have eaten their fill, the birds fly away.

We invite birds to the garden, but our hospitality has so far never been reciprocated. We have been willing to overlook this minor shortcoming since their tiny nests aren't large enough to accommodate human visitors.

I swept the snails, slugs, and long brown worms off the veranda and also washed off the bird droppings. By means of excrement, the birds had protested against our delay in providing them with their long-awaited morning meal. It had taken me years to understand this simple message. If only they had the power of speech, how these birds would have scolded us for our negligence!

When a distant bell began to strike eight, I started preparing breakfast. The work took about forty minutes to get ready, which seems a long time in view of the fact that the majority need only about ten minutes for this purpose. Actually, within five minutes, one can either make several slices of buttered toast with jam or fill a bowl with cornflakes and boil some milk for it. Often, breakfast consists only of a strong cup of coffee because people are hard-pressed for time. Little wonder that their health is never good. In a world that is becoming increasingly polluted with every day that passes, is it a waste of time to think about what is safest to eat and drink? It *does* take time to produce health-giving dishes.

Our two-course meal is nourishing and substantial, so much so that it gives us enough energy up to lunchtime. But twice a week we skip lunch, regarding this practice of food deprivation for short periods as fasts of sorts.

In restaurants, it is the guests who are kept waiting until the food arrives, but in our home, it is the breakfast on the table that has to wait for us. The dishes are deferred until we are ready. In order of priority, yoga comes first, breakfast afterwards. An empty tummy is best for yoga.

In the privacy of our home and on a comfortable yoga mattress, I did nearly forty minutes of yoga. There were spinal, intestinal, and various other postures of immense benefit to the entire body and mind. To ensure the free and easy movement of the limbs without any obstacle whatsoever, I did the exercises in the nude. But I remembered to be fully clothed when I went out in the open air for doing ten minutes of deep breathing exercises. We agree that all human beings, without exception, were born bare, but who wants to offend the prim and proper with prying eyes? Anyway, anyone who cares to inhale pure air deeply can oxygenate, regenerate, and reinvigorate the entire system. Claudia followed suit but not unclad, being somewhat influenced by her Protestant and puritanical upbringing. She spent a lot of time under a pine tree doing her breathing exercises, *Pranayama*, while communing with nature.

While having breakfast we talked occasionally, but most of the time we were silent; we slowly masticated the food. Some birds made high-pitched noises. Then two of them broke into a shrill. But all these sounds were not a nuisance by any means. If anything, they were music to our ears.

Suddenly we heard the doorbell ringing. I walked along the granite pathway to the gate on Chemin du Colombier. What did I see? Three children—two girls dressed up as witches and a boy in the garb of a ghost—were standing there, all wearing dark pointed hats with black marks all over their babyish faces. They were smiling broadly. Their merry mood made them scream. The tiny baskets they carried were for collecting chocolates and other delicacies.

"Bonjour!" the kids shouted in unison.

Only then did I realise that the children were celebrating Halloween. When I invited them in, they all ran into the living room and seated themselves on chairs. They introduced themselves to Claudia by telling her their forenames and the surnames of their parents. She rose to the occasion by filling their baskets with biscuits, sweets, cakes, and fruits. They all looked contented.

"We're going to the next house," said the boy-ghost as they left in a hurry.

During the special silent spell of the day that ranged from around 9 a.m. when we finished breakfast to 2 p.m. when we began lunch, we remained incommunicado. We not only cut ourselves off from the outer world by disconnecting the telephone and not using the computer to send or receive emails, but also isolated ourselves from each other. In other words, I made no attempt to get into a conversation with Claudia nor did she try to do the same with me. Undisturbed, we were able to do some creative work. We realised once again that for creative writing quietude and solitude are best. Some of this precious time was also devoted to reading. I was able to go through the complicated details in some of my manuscripts that required all my undivided attention. In this atmosphere of stillness, I was also able to do nothing and give my mind a rest.

The grey clouds drifted away and it was no longer gloomy. There was bright sunshine instead. We decided to sit on the wooden bench under the enormous pine tree. We had to turn in a north-easterly direction to avoid the piercing glare of the sun. One of the blessings in our region, the south-east of France, is that we can enjoy spells of sunny summer-like weather in the midst of autumn. We felt that we were extremely lucky. The clement climate of Les Arcs-sur-Argens is often pleasant.

Claudia brought out the lunch on a large tray to a shady spot under the tree. The meal she had prepared was simple but delectable; it was mostly organic food. I ate a plateful of boiled rice with curried lentils. It was supplemented with steamed broccoli and French beans. I particularly liked the side dish of grated carrots and garlic mixed with chopped parsley and olive oil. For dessert, we enjoyed a few fresh dates from Tunisia. Eating outdoors, weather permitting, is excellent for relaxation.

We followed the time-honoured custom of the locals of taking a siesta soon after lunch or at a suitable hour in the afternoon. Our siestas never lasted more than twenty minutes. Based on bitter experience, I knew that sleepless nights could sometimes be caused by long siestas. On the day in question, just fifteen minutes were sufficient to have forty winks. I think there isn't any hard and fast rule on this matter. Let the body decide how long it desires to stay in bed!

Soon after a good siesta, I have always had a wonderful sense of well-being. A siesta breaks the day; it is a welcome intermission for persons from all walks of life, especially for those who have to toil in the soil or for people who suffer from the wear and tear of stressful work indoors. Siestas never fail to recharge our mental and physical batteries.

It was quite warm for late October.

"I'd love to walk on the beach in Saint Raphael," I said.

"Let's make a dash for the station," said Claudia. "The train leaves in thirty minutes."

We locked the house and set off on foot for the Les Arcs railway station. It was a mad dash for the ticket office.

"Thanks to our brisk pace, we've arrived in time," I panted.

While travelling on the train, I closed my eyes to take a breather.

The sight of lovely long stretches of green vineyards was

uplifting. The train passed by fields and stables. Horses were grazing on grass. The only passenger in our compartment was a teenager with his eyes glued to his laptop. Perhaps he was doing his homework or playing computer games. How he spent his time was his business. However, it was a pity that he never raised his head and cast even a fleeting glance at the beautiful scenery outside.

In times past, passengers in trains, buses, and aeroplanes would read books while travelling. Those days there were no electronic toys or new fangled gadgets to occupy their minds. Nowadays, rare is the sight of travellers engrossed in books. The younger generation doesn't seem to know the joy of collecting, owning, touching, and above all, reading books. Poor things, I only wish they knew what they were missing. Their parents probably failed to introduce them to the joy of reading fairy stories when they were kids. Losing oneself in a fantasy world helps to develop the imagination. Filling the impressionable minds of boys and girls with scientific and technical information is not enough, parents and teachers must also go out of their way to stimulate creativity in the young.

What a charming seaside! At first, the long beach seemed deserted. There arose a certain sadness when it dawned on me that the summer was no more. The beach used to be clean and tidy during the warm season. Now it was badly maintained. A litter of plastic bags, empty bottles, and newspapers were all strewn on the sand. Even so, the beach was not without its beauty.

Two young men with strained expressions were jogging; a few children were shouting and playing football; a muscular man and a scantily clad woman were laughing loudly and walking arm in arm; an elderly man and his grandson were fishing; a boy was struggling to fly his kite on this windless day. A lady was filming her tiny granddaughter as she splashed in the surf; this five-year-old girl looked rather ridiculous in a bra.

After having rolled our trousers up, we slowly walked along the beach, remembering to scrape our toes against the sand. This practice, according to the advice of a friend who practised naturopathy, was extremely beneficial to the entire body. It certainly helped to polish up the toenails and give the feet a good massage. Before long, we suddenly realised that we had been strolling on the beach for nearly forty minutes, going all the way from Saint Raphael to the neighbouring town of Fréjus. It was too late in the day to visit the archaeological sites of the ancient Roman settlement of Fréjus. We sat on a sand dune, giving our tired limbs a good long stretch. So soft and comfortable was the warm sand that we allowed ourselves to sink deeper and deeper into it. The whole night could have been spent there, especially because this nice spot could not be easily seen by other people strolling along the beach. All I could see was the bluish-green waters of the vast Mediterranean. I was fascinated by the sharply defined and unbroken line of the horizon. These conditions were conducive to quiet contemplation, all the more because I was unexpectedly able to forget my day-to-day matters and think instead about questions of perennial interest.

Twilight had not yet set in; the skies were clear and it was still easy to see. In the far distance, a motor-boat stood out in silhouette. While lying on the sand, I gazed into the heavens. As I continued to gaze into space, it struck me that space is both without a beginning and an end. Then I visualised a conversation with an imaginary astronomer.

"I've explored the universe until I saw the very edge of space," he boasted.

"That's all very well, but what's on the other side of the edge?" I asked to satisfy my curiosity.

"You want to know what's on the other side," he replied with a furrowed brow. "I suppose it can't be anything other than space itself."

Space is limitless; it is without a beginning and an end. And so is time. Time has neither a beginning nor an end. If someone were to tell me that time came into existence on such and such a date, I would immediately counter that assertion by posing this question: "What had been there *before* that date?"

For the reason that the universe had always been there, in one form or another, changing but still continuing, would it be reasonable to conclude that the universe was the handiwork of a creator? Is not the creator the creation of man's fertile imagination?

We are full of self-importance, not realising that we are

only insignificant specks of dust, even smaller than dust, in this incalculably immense universe. We have neither the power nor the ability to change the world, let alone the universe, but we can at least meditate on our unimportance, deflate the ego, and thus change our inner nature.

We walked briskly along the restaurant-lined road bordering the seashore, rushing all the way from Fréjus back to Saint Raphael to be in good time for the train. Just as we arrived there, an officer of the SNCF declared, "The train to Les Arcs is delayed for fifty minutes. A big tree has fallen on the track. Merci de votre compréhension—thanks for your understanding."

With time to kill, we went into a splendid cathedral nearby—Notre-Dame-de-Victoire (a cathedral from 1884)—with a conspicuous golden statue of the Virgin at the entrance. The cathedral's beautiful dome was reminiscent of Russian churches and Byzantine architecture. We crept into the imposing structure and sat in a pew without causing any disturbance. The faithful were at evening Mass. Although we are not Christians, let alone Catholics, the sublime experience of hearing a spirited chanting of Schubert's Ave Maria was quite moving.

Inside the train, we made conversation with Marianne, a lady in her late forties who had several children. They all live in Les Arcs. A woman with a stern face, Marianne, I knew, was a churchgoer.

"The other day you saw my husband, but you didn't say bonjour to him," she complained.

"That's possible," I replied. "Probably my mind was a little preoccupied."

"But you *should* have said bonjour," she repeated in an accusing tone.

"In life what's important is to have *no* hate," I remarked. "Whether or not you care to greet people is unimportant. Often the well-mannered are only making a show."

On Marianne's face, there was a forced smile. I could tell that she was not pleased with my comment.

On our arrival at the Les Arcs railway station, I found the place unusually crowded. Outside the station, because of the toxic fumes that their cigarettes gave off, the few who smoked were annoying the many who didn't. The right to breathe air that is fresh, clean, and unpolluted should surely be incorporated into the charter of human rights.

Passengers were getting into their cars. There were hardly any taxis. Claudia and I had to wade through the heavy traffic until we reached the narrow pathway leading to the quiet plateau where we lived.

It was late. Claudia was fatigued; it was not possible to cook any special dishes. Yet, the tasty dinner she prepared consisted of pasta and cabbage curry. Afterwards, we had two red organic apples and dried prunes.

To unwind before going to bed, we listened to music by Joseph Haydn. It was his symphony titled *Lamentatione*.

Had we not been so worn out, we would have followed our normal practice of doing ten minutes of meditation. We usually sit on a carpet in a dark room and close our eyes. Then we passively watch the thought process in motion, without interfering in any way with the free flow of thoughts and feelings, until the mind quietens down of its own accord. Then the inner train comes to a halt.

The night was beautiful. The crescent moon stood out in the star-studded sky. The few stars that I was familiar with were in their right places, so to speak! Just seeing them there, strangely enough, gave me a certain sense of security.

In the course of this chapter, I have described in detail my lifestyle in the belief that my way of living might, directly or indirectly, inspire some at least, to lead a contemplative and meditative life. Having quit the rat race, which is concerned with the mundane, I have now the time and good health that are necessary to delve into the spiritual.

What are my concluding remarks?

While living in a stressful society, how many are able to comprehend the conditioning influences that have hitherto kept them in bondage? Today, unfortunately, few are interested in fully unwinding their minds that are wrapped in psychological problems of their own making. Unwinding the mind is the only door leading to the celestial sphere of clarity. We can call it clear-sightedness as it enables the enlightened few to perceive what is true or real. They become a beacon of hope and guidance to the rest of society.

These rare and advanced adepts stand out in our world that is fast becoming more and more insane because of man's craving for power, position, prestige, and prosperity. They alone, being replete with clarity, are blessed with palpable peace of mind and heartfelt happiness.

ACKNOWLEDGEMENT

I must express my gratitude to several persons, especially the invisible beings who inspire and help me when I write.

Claudia Weeraperuma made invaluable suggestions and corrections.

I am particularly thankful to Gayatri Goswami, who carefully edited the entire manuscript and improved it.

Finally, Shikha Sabharwal's boldness in publishing an unconventional book that challenges long cherished views deserves praise.

Susunaga Weeraperuma, who lives in the quietness of a medieval village called Les Arcs-sur-Argens in the south of France, devotes his time to *hatha* yoga, *pranayama*, organic gardening, creative writing, reading, and meditation. He is a pacifist, a vegetarian, an animal rights activist, a connoisseur of art, a classical music buff, and a traveller. This prolific author's wide variety of publications range from entertaining short stories and novels to in-depth studies of religion, Buddhist philosophy, J. Krishnamurti's teachings, and meditation. Of late, he has been writing books of essays, like the present one, that are self-searching in character.